The NQTeachers' Survival Guide
(2nd edition)

HAZEL BENNETT

Published by Edgware Books

© Hazel Bennett 2014

www.edgware-books.co.uk

First published by Edgware Books in 2013
2nd Edition 2014

Front cover © Hazel Bennett
ISBN: 978-0-9574648-6-5

To Graham, Russell, Alicia, Michael, Aimee, Aidan,
Henry and Kathryn

To the many thousands of pupils who have given me so
much pleasure and satisfaction.

THE NQTEACHERS' SURVIVAL GUIDE

CONTENTS

ACKNOWLEDGEMENTS

I should like to thank these teachers for their helpful contributions to The NQTeachers' Survival Guide.

Russell Bennett	Thomas Bleakley
Sue Brown	Debby Cohen
Carole Edwards	Fiona Eldridge
Gene Henderson	Emma Laikin
Joan Little	Kendal Maouchi
Samantha Nye	Catherine Paynter
Judy Sitton	Frances Smith
Renee Stanton	Cecilia Stevenson

With special thanks to the author, Kate Nivison, for her expert advice.

HAZEL BENNETT

FOREWORD

Teaching is an interesting, stimulating and rewarding job. Though the salaries are not high in the lower echelons, they are still higher than in nursing, and in some cases, architects and junior doctors. If you reach the top and become a headteacher, you can earn over £100,000 in some inner city schools, though you will earn every penny of it if you do. Some Education Authorities are so desperately short of headteachers that they give their most successful heads two schools to run for a high salary.

It is a job which is full of challenges, exciting and inspiring for those with creative, inventive minds. For those who succeed, there is the reward of knowing you have guided pupils towards the ladder of success and most people remember, with affection and gratitude, teachers who inspired them or guided them towards a satisfying career. Of course, the holidays are an added bonus.

So why are some areas of the country constantly short of teachers? Why are there often masses of vacancies which stay unfilled, in spite of the fact that the nation's universities send out more and more teachers every year? Why do so many teachers, who enter the profession filled with enthusiasm and the urge to succeed, fall by the wayside within the first few years, their expensive and hard won qualifications wasted? Teaching has its pitfalls.

Teachers spend a vast number of hours on tasks other than actual classroom teaching and this tends to wear them out and distract them from the real job of enthusing the nation's pupils.

Preparing lesson plans in ever more copious and unnecessary detail and keeping progressively more detailed notes is tiring and time-consuming. Reading new government documents and being disheartened by the regular changes which are imposed as soon as you have become accustomed to the last one is irritating. When exam results are announced politicians shout that the rise in grades represents a fall in standards, in spite of the Examining Boards' protests that they have observed a definite rise.

Coping with a pupil population, who are increasingly aware of their rights and not always assuming the same need to consider their responsibilities or other children's rights, can at times be soul destroying, especially when you've spent valuable time trying to make lessons as appealing as possible.

We all know that competent teachers who can inspire their pupils to want to learn and ultimately become contributing adults are vital to the well-being of the nation. Of course our pupils deserve happy, stable schools where they can thrive and succeed. And who isn't aware that schools cannot deliver the best unless they are fully staffed and supported by management, parents and government?

Becoming an enthusiastic teacher, who can rise above the difficulties and inspire pupils to succeed, is a mammoth task but the rewards of job satisfaction and pleasure are just as great. The objective of this handbook is to offer NQTs guidance in identifying the difficulties and to point out ways to rise above them, and hopefully encourage teachers to stay in the profession.

1   Starting off on the right foot

In recent years, teacher training has become more school based. This leaves training providers with fewer days to turn graduates into teachers. This book gives you the nitty-gritty which lecturers have not got time to tell you.

Don't be surprised if you have first day jitters. After all your hard work at college, this can be a very exciting time. Don't be surprised if you feel your stomach quivering on the first day, because many newly qualified teachers do. For some teachers, the first time alone at the chalk face is nerve-wracking. Schools can be a hot-house of pressure with which you must learn to deal in order to survive. Some teachers have a terrible time in their first year, leave the profession and never teach again. Fortunately many, who suffer all sorts of initial difficulties, rise above them, emerge with confidence and proceed to have satisfying and successful careers.

The most testing part is coping with a longer working day than you were used to at college, and then going home to more school-related work. Even today, when NQTs have shorter contact hours than in the past, you have to cope with classes all day for the first time, and the stress of this is tiring, leaving you less able to manage the extra hours.

If you work with a lot of experienced teachers, it can be unnerving as you watch them cope with ease. I have known young teachers to feel threatened in these circumstances and try to put on an air of confidence or pretend to know more than they did. This is unwise because the facade falls apart eventually and then teachers are less sympathetic. Always ask for help or information if you need it. No one can blame you for being willing to learn. Don't be afraid to admit to your colleagues that you are nervous. They were once nervous NQTs and they will probably sympathize and be all the more supportive.

The workload

In the weeks that follow, the list of daily tasks increases until you'll find yourself inundated. Your success in passing the induction year is commensurate with your ability to handle the large workload. It is important to prioritize. When you feel you cannot get everything done, write down every task that needs doing and number them in order of importance. Start working through the list and as soon as your head begins to ache, stop working. If you can't manage it all, leave the last tasks.

As long as you have put the planning in on time and prepared the lessons, you can probably postpone a few jobs. It is never worth persevering when you are tired because you make mistakes and become so tired and stressed that your performance level drops.

Teaching is very dehydrating so it is sensible to go to the staffroom for a drink every break-time when you are not on playground duty. It is not a waste of time because the break and the drink also help you to unwind if you have had a difficult session. It is an opportunity to build relationships with your colleagues. Don't try to be an island. You need their support.

NQTs are frequently enthusiastic about taking on extra responsibilities. Do resist the temptation to start an after school club in the first year. It takes about a year to establish a routine of planning, preparing, delivering lessons and marking efficiently. No one will think you lazy if you postpone the extra-curricular activities until the second year, or the summer term at least.

Dos and don'ts

The ship only sails smoothly if all are pulling their weight and leaning in the same direction. Regular staff absences or crew members out of kilter with the rest of the group lead to the burdens being increased on some crew members, a slowing down of progress and a few ructions along the way.

The first rule is don't create waves. Teachers, who have been in a school for many years, don't want the place reorganized in line with the latest thinking on education. I knew an NQT, who spent her first six months suggesting ways in which experienced teachers could improve their performance, and then couldn't understand why no one bothered to speak to her. Another failed his first year of teaching and had it extended, mostly because he inadvertently antagonized his mentor with his strong views. If you have ideas for reforming and improving the school, save them for your second year.

When the going gets tough, it is tempting to take a bit of time off, especially as this is so easy in days when you can sign yourself off for a week without a doctor's certificate. Try not to do it more than a two or three times during the whole year. Teachers accept a certain amount of this from NQTs but their patience runs out eventually. It will be noticed if you malinger on days when it is your turn to take assembly, or your lessons are due to be monitored. Everybody assumes these are the reasons for your absence and it does your credibility more harm than turning up and under-performing.

Seize every opportunity to escape to the NQTs' Inset, during class time. It may become the best break you have in the week. When the older teachers in the staffroom enviously tell you how lucky you are because they didn't have any of that in their youth, smile sympathetically and say nothing.

The cast and crew

I was once in a school which had a very successful Ofsted. The inspectors noted that there were harmonious, respectful relationships between all ranks of staff and attributed some our success to teamwork.

NQTs should not underestimate the value of getting on with the team. For your own comfort, try to establish a positive relationship with everyone. Also, pupils of all ages are quick to notice if the teachers and support staff do not support each other and they will be quick to get through the cracks.

Know your cast and crew and their roles and how to interact with them. It is vital to keep them on your side. These include:

- the head;

- the school governors;
- teachers;
- teaching assistants;
- the non-teaching staff - secretaries, schoolkeeper, cleaners, kitchen staff
- volunteers.

The head

Being a headteacher is arguably the most difficult role in teaching. Most people involved, i.e. the teachers, non-teaching staff, the pupils, the parents, the governors and the inspectors all tend to suggest shooting the head for all that is not going well. Those who are most eager to blame the head are the least likely to give him/her credit for all that does go well.

Headteachers' responsibilities increase annually and the number, who suffer nervous breakdowns or retire early with stress, is on the increase. With a double helping of pressure and power, it is not surprising that they tend to be rather an autocratic bunch.

Some say they are willing to be democratic and allow the staff to have a free vote in decision making, but usually they only do so on issues where they do not have strong preferences. I have even known a head to allow a vote but, when he didn't win, he ignored the vote and did what he wanted to do anyway.

A few tips

- In the first month, the head will regularly wander past your room and peer through the window in your door to see how you are faring. Find a large poster to cover the window before you start.

- The head will probably ask how you are managing. Smile confidently and say, 'Fine, thank you.' If s/he thinks you are having difficulty, s/he will scrutinise you more closely. If you have any difficulties, take them to your mentor.
- If the head asks you to go on courses during your own time, refuse apologetically saying you need the time for planning and preparation.
- If the head chases you up about some job you have left undone, smile apologetically, and say, 'Thank you for reminding me. I have it as my first priority to attend to after today's marking, tomorrow's preparation and my appointment with Jimmy's mother.'
- Some heads are inclined to resent teachers who appear to question their judgement. Never ask, 'Why have we got to do.......?' Instead ask, 'Can you please explain the thinking behind........'
- It's not worth crossing swords with the head in your first year because you could not possibly win.

The school governors

The system of school management is quite unlike any other institution. Each school has a committee of governors, which includes the head, representatives of the teachers, non-teaching staff and parents, some local business persons, representatives of the Local Education Authority and the church or synagogue, if it is a denominational school. The number depends on the size of the school. In other words, people, who are not well-educated and know nothing about running a school, can vote against the head, as can junior members of staff, secretaries or dinner ladies if they are governors.

The parents, teachers and non-teaching staff are proposed as candidates, frequently by themselves, and seconded by one other, and then elected by their peers and pals. Many parents are not interested and in some schools only a tiny per centage bothers to vote. One of my friends proposed himself as a parent governor, was seconded by his wife and elected unopposed.

Understandably, this system frequently astonishes teachers from abroad who are amazed that people who have little knowledge of education can have power over the head.

The governors' tasks include interviewing and selecting staff, overseeing the budget, granting permission for pupils to be permanently excluded, hearing appeals of pupils who have been suspended or excluded, rubber-stamping promotion of staff and payments to staff on the upper pay spine or dealing with their appeals. In practice, many act on the advice of the head.

Governors are a much maligned group of people and, like the rest of us, they vary enormously. Some governors, who are retired, or are full-time housewives/husbands are like gold dust to their school when they spend a day per week in school, helping in classrooms, going on school trips, running the school library and organising fund-raising events. Others rarely darken the door of the place during the school day, don't know the staff, and do very little for the establishment.

Headteachers sometimes have ambivalent attitudes to them. If the governors are not well-educated, professional people, they resent having to obtain their approval and apply to them for their pay rise, permission to permanently exclude a child and make a variety of changes. If they are well-educated, professional people of some social standing, sometimes heads resent being scrutinised by articulate, confident people who can stand up to them and question their decisions instead of automatically rubber-stamping them as the former type would normally do.

Some teachers complain that the governors do not come into school often enough and then don't bother to make them welcome when they do, so it is worth cultivating their goodwill by making them feel welcome. The more they feel appreciated the harder they will work for the school.

If they are parents, you will probably have their child in your class one day, and they will support you better if you have already developed a friendly working relationship with them. If you apply for a post of responsibility, you may have to face them across the interview table. Remember that if you intend to stay in the school for years, they also make the final decision, based on the headteacher's advice, about whether you receive later increments on the upper pay spine.

It is rare for governors to give individual teachers any problems but a few do not understand the parameters of their roles. Individual governors do not have any real power over individual teachers. If you think a governor is imposing on you unreasonably, a tactful answer is, 'I'm not sure if I can do that. I'll have to ask the head's permission,' and follow it through.

If you think they are not making the correct decisions, the only real solution is for you to stand for election and be a teacher governor yourself.

Being a school governor is a thankless task. They are not paid for their trouble, and are sometimes resented. Not surprisingly, it is usually very easy to become a governor, because most schools have difficulty in finding enough people for the job.

If you do join a governing body, it is important to go on a training course to have a clear view of the extent of your responsibilities and the limitations of your power.

It is also important to make it a priority to attend every monthly meeting. I have known a variety of heads who suffered great frustration caused by governors who regularly failed to turn up because they had something better to do. Likewise it is vital to carry out any task accepted, quickly and efficiently.

Teachers

Your mentor

To help you to stay on top of it all, you will have a mentor, an experienced member of staff, who has been allocated the task of showing you how to cut your teeth. It is wise to form a positive working relationship with him or her, because s/he can encourage you and guide you through the difficulties, or undermine you until you give up.

Some mentors mother NQTs through their first year. Others do little for them. If you do have a mentor with whom you cannot get on, approach the senior member of staff with whom you have the best relationship and explain your problems in a purely factual manner, being careful not to create acrimony. In extreme cases, the head will change the mentor, but only if you have a good case.

Always let your mentor see that you value their support. Don't be afraid to ask questions, or admit that you do not know something. Mentors do not expect NQTs to know everything and no one can blame you for being eager to learn.

Other teachers

You should also try to form a friendly relationship with all teachers in the group, as they can support and encourage you through the fray.

- Always be civil to the ambitious teachers on the staff. One of them might be your head, one day.
- Be equally kind to the unambitious teachers. They will keep you sane when end of term pressure invades the school.
- If you are an ambitious teacher, be respectful to everyone, because next year, when you have a post of responsibility, they will be much less co-operative if you have spent your induction year irritating them.
- If you are not an ambitious teacher, it's fine to stay that way. Many teachers do an excellent job without climbing the career ladder.

Support Teachers

Teachers of English as an additional language (EAL) and Special Educational Needs (SEN)

Every class has its little group of children who need extra support, and in many schools, particularly in cities, there is a growing number of pupils who enter the school with very little English. Support teachers are invaluable in helping you to cope.

They normally work in the classroom with you. Some

teachers dislike having another teacher in their room, 'watching' them and try to get the support teacher to take a group of pupils out. Don't feel anxious about their presence. They are there to support you, not to inspect you.

If it is the school's policy for the support teacher to take pupils outside the classroom to work, then talk to the teacher about what they are doing in the lesson. If appropriate, ask them to do a differentiated version of what you are doing in class. Be aware that the more you work in unison, the more the support teacher will feel appreciated and the more it will benefit your pupils.

Support teachers will have more expertise with EAL or SEN pupils than you. Some NQTs try to appear to know it all. This does not fool their more experienced colleagues and it decreases their goodwill. If you let them see that you value their expertise and want to learn from them they will be more proactive in helping you.

In order to make things run smoothly and get most benefit from them, try these.

- Plan to have the most complicated lessons of the week when they are in your classroom.
- Invite them to planning meetings for the lessons which they will teach with you, but do not mind if they cannot come because they have to work in a lot of different classes.
- If they cannot come to the planning meeting, go over the plan with them, in advance, making it clear what you want them to do with their EAL/SEN pupils.
- Show that you value their expertise by asking them for suggestions to achieve the objective with their focus group.

- Some teachers try to use their support teacher as a cover teacher to release themselves from the class. Try never to do this because it causes ill feeling and does not benefit the children who most need support.
- In many schools, support teachers have to write an evaluation on how each lesson went. If this is the case, then make sure you read it, because it irritates them if they find out that you haven't.
- When you see the pupils' exam/assessment/ SATs results, always acknowledge the support teachers' help if their focus pupils have made good progress.
- If they have given you a lot of support, then, at the end of each term, show your appreciation with a bottle of wine or a letter of thanks in their pigeon hole.

Teaching assistants (TAs)

Teaching assistants are a luxury for which we never dared to hope in the 70s and 80s. As well as teaching small groups, they do light, behind-the-scenes jobs, like saving the class teacher from having a nervous breakdown. If treated kindly, they will put up your classroom displays, do your photocopying, nip out of class to fetch the resources you have forgotten, sharpen the pencils and all the irritating chores. It is wise to give them a lot of encouragement and gratitude, as they can be a wonderful source of support.

In recent years, the quality of classroom teaching assistants has risen steadily. They now take training courses for which they have to do assignments to get a certificate. Some do advanced training and achieve Higher Level Teaching Assistant (HLTA) status, and they are allowed to take the class while teachers have their planning, preparation and assessment time (PPA).

I have known them to have degrees and even a qualified teacher who worked as a classroom assistant because she wanted an easier life. Never ask them to mind the class for you unless they are qualified to do so. It's taking unfair advantage of them and they will support you much better if you treat them fairly. Life was much harder without them.

A few tips

- Treat them with the same respect that you give your mentor and the head. Let them see that you value their expertise.
- Give them a copy of the plan for each lesson for which they will be in your class. Before the lesson, take the time to go over it in detail and make them feel involved, because they also take pride in their work.
- Make sure the pupils treat them with the same respect which you would expect them to give to other teachers.
- Always pass on to them, anything positive which anyone says about their work.
- Encourage them to go on courses. The more they know the more they can help you.

The non-teaching staff

School secretaries
They will know every error you make on the school registers and requisition forms. Irritate them, and all your misdemeanours will be relayed to the head.

A very small number are bossy and think they can order NQTs around. Do not fall for it. Smile and look them in the eye and speak calmly. Let them see you are not threatened by their manner. If you are not happy with what they are telling you to do, give answers like, 'I'll just check that with my mentor,' and follow it through. Fortunately most are helpful and pleasant.

School caretakers
They should be handled with care. The speed with which they fix anything broken in your classroom or fetch heavy bits of equipment, is often in direct proportion to the kindness you have previously shown them. When s/he moans at you about what a raw deal s/he always gets, look sympathetic and say nothing. A small number are bossy and awkward.

Never let them push you about. Be polite but firm, with answers like, 'I'll have to check that with the head,' and follow it up. Report intimidating behaviour to the head at once, with expressions like. 'He appeared to be threatening...' Happily the last piece of advice is rarely needed.

Cleaners
Always speak kindly to whoever cleans your classroom because you may need to ask her/him to keep an eye out for small pieces of apparatus that go missing during the day. I have found that a box of chocolates at Christmas

works wonders.

Be careful what you say to other teachers if there is cleaner within earshot. I knew one who tried to cause trouble by repeating a teacher's comments about a child to the child's mother. If you find any member of the auxiliary staff behaving like this report it to your mentor or the head at once.

The kitchen staff

If the school meals are edible, and some aren't, it is worth being pleasant to the kitchen staff and throwing in the occasional compliment to the cook. You get a higher level of service, and larger portions of food if you are in favour with them.

Also, when you keep children in at lunch-time to finish their work and you inadvertently release them after they stop serving, they are less likely to complain to the head when you ask them to stop clearing up and provide the child with his lunch.

Volunteers

In some schools, parents and others like to come into school for a day or so per week to help teachers by hearing children read and other tasks. They can be a great help but you must be careful, because they are not members of staff and they may gossip about the school to parents.

Make them welcome and show that you appreciate their help but check with your mentor if they are allowed into the staffroom. If not, bring them a cup of tea at break-time and sit in the classroom and chat to them. Some may try to draw you into a conversation about children, but be careful never tell them anything about any pupil other than their own child.

If you take parent volunteers on a school trip, and sometimes you cannot manage without them, make sure you make them aware of all the safety regulations. At the end of the day, either invite them in for a cup of tea or write them a letter of thanks for the effort they have put in to help you.

Although there is a ranking system in every school, the schools where all staff treat everyone with equal kindness and respect are the ones which have the happiest atmosphere and often the best standards of pupil behaviour.

2 The parents

Always start with the premise that parents and teachers both want the children to be happy and succeed, and so they should be on the same side, supporting each other. Usually parents and teachers maintain a friendly relationship which benefits the child and promotes a positive attitude to school work.

Some NQTs are wary of parents. This is understandable because in a small minority of cases, they can be a never-ending source of grief. Alternately, they can halve your difficulties and be a constant source of support. It is as important to treat them with care as it is the pupils. Always remember that you are dealing with their most precious possession and so allow for a modicum of rose-coloured judgment on their part.

Like their children, they vary enormously. There is no need ever to feel threatened by parents who are themselves teachers. I have often found them quite sympathetic, because they understand the difficulties with which you have to cope. Many are a tremendous bonus. If they come on school trips they know exactly what is expected of them and do not wander off to the café or the pub, unlike some who think they have been invited because you wanted to treat them to a day out.

Try to avoid confrontations with parents because they often lead to more problems than they solve. As with pupils, never back them into a corner, otherwise they will come out fighting. Try to give them an escape route and keep their goodwill because you have to teach their child until the end of the year or longer in secondary school. You may also have to teach their siblings in later years so it is worth keeping the path smooth.

If you teach in an independent school, you will find parents who will support their children's education to the hilt. If you tell them that their child is not putting in his/her best effort, they will support you at once, provided, of course, that you make your comments in a calm manner making it clear that you are concerned about the child's progress, not delivering a complaint. If they are not happy about their child's progress, they will let you know very quickly and expect you to do something about it at once.

In independent schools, parents take the attitude that they are paying and so, like the piper, they should call the tune. This sounds reasonable to many, but it is impractical because they have different views and it is impossible to please them all. In the same class you can have some parents telling you to give more homework and others telling you to give less or none. Headteachers are more wary of standing up to parents in independent schools because the establishment is a business and the parent is a paying customer. Some take the view, like the managers of department stores, that the customer is always right and they are less likely to support you than a state school head.

When parents see new teachers they sometimes target them. When a parent in an independent school demands that you change your ways, it is best to say that you are following school policy and direct them to the head or the appropriate senior member of staff if they wish to bring about change.

Building a positive relationship

Think ahead. When you receive your class list(s) for the following year, start looking out for the new parents and approach them with a comment like, 'I'm having your Freddie in my class, next year. (Smile and look pleased about it, especially if you aren't). Do pop in and see me occasionally to see how he's getting on.'

You'll be amazed how far a little bit of goodwill goes. Of course, if you work in a school where the parents don't have jobs outside the home and want to stay for an hour on a regular basis, ignore this point.

Some of these might help.

- It's important to start on the right foot. On first meeting parents always start warm and friendly. Let them see you as a kindly person, interested in their child.
- Get to know their names as soon as you can. If they are step-parents or have a different name from the pupil, try to get it right. They appreciate that.
- Some families have complicated lives. The 'father' is occasionally a live-in partner. Try to be sensitive, and stay in touch with the real father as well.
- Many pupils live with carers. I have always tried especially hard to build a good relationship with them because these pupils need most support.
- It's best to be approachable, not aloof. Always smile, speak or nod if you run into them.
- Make sure the child realizes that you see his parents

as your friends.

- Parents don't like surprises. If there is a change of plan or procedure, make sure you tell them in advance. If a pupil is absent long-term, it is well worth a phone-call and they will appreciate your making the effort.

- Make sure you tell parents what you expect from pupils – homework in on time, politeness, punctuality etc. Explain or remind them of the school policy on any issue where there is disagreement. Use expressions like, 'As I'm sure you are aware, the school's policy on this is ...'

- If they say your demands are unreasonable, explain the reason for them and the possible consequences of their child's action.

- Be a good listener.

- Try to avoid confrontations. Humour often works.

- Never let a parent know if you dislike their child.

- On first meeting parents, if they look tense, or their child has a track record of misbehaviour, greet them with a smile and say, 'Ah yes, he's a likeable lad, isn't he,' (primary). Another useful expression is, 'I quite like your son because he is....' and mention a few of his good points. (secondary)

- If they are becoming argumentative, turn the conversation round by asking the questions like: 'What do you think are his/her weaknesses/strengths?'
  'Does s/he do this at home?'
  'How do you deal with it at home?'
  It is a non-aggressive way of guiding them to acknowledge their child's less endearing qualities.

- Record details of all meetings in case it has to be referred to later. If the parent is known to be difficult, make sure they see you scribbling notes and your writing is illegible upside down.

- If you work in a school where parents are pushy or quick to complain, it is worth lingering in the playground for about fifteen minutes after school and having a friendly chat with a different parent each afternoon. Letting them see that you are interested in them breaks down aggression.

Dealing with difficulties

- When you have a worse than average difficulty with a child, it is wise to call in the support of parents before the problem grows. If you leave it a long time until, say, parents' night, they will give you the answer, 'If s/he's been giving you that much difficulty you should have told me much sooner so that I could sort it out.'

- Explain your problem in a calm, factual manner. Try to keep negative adjectives out of it, in the first instance at least.

- If a child settles down and improves after you have spoken to the parents, look out for them and tell them how pleased you are. Thank them for their support. They need reassurance too and a simple word of thanks builds a bridge for the future. Remember, you might get one of their other children in a future year.

- Never verbally attack parents even if they attack you first. Stay calm, stick to facts – they speak louder than insults - and do not let the conversation deteriorate into a slanging match.

- If you have a problem, start positively by saying something like, 'I feel I really need your help here. Your son is a lovely, polite boy and he tries hard with his work. I like having him in my French class but can you please remind him to bring in his homework book each Friday because I haven't seen it for a fortnight.'

- If they won't listen to you or let you get a word in, wait until they have finished, smile and say politely, never sarcastically, 'I have listened to you patiently for ten minutes. Will you please listen to me now for the same time without interrupting?' If they still won't listen, finish the meeting immediately.

Parents' Consultation Evenings

Most schools have one, two or three per year. You have between five and fifteen minutes to establish a positive relationship, inform parents of their child's progress and answer their queries. NQTs and even some experienced teachers and parents have also told me they are nervous.

Preparing for the evening

- Forewarned is fore-armed! In a primary school, have a chat with the previous class teacher and find out, in advance, if any parents are likely to be difficult and in what way. In a secondary school, ask the class's previous form teacher.
- Look again at the Home and School policy, to remind yourself of its details. Have one in your drawer. It is handy to have it available to back up your comments if the parents are argumentative.
- It is difficult to keep all the information in your head, so make notes on any issues you have to raise.

- Clear all the untidy heaps off your desk and replace them with all your record books so that you have information at hand if needed.
- Stop the last lesson of the afternoon ¼ hour early to tidy up the classroom. Give each child a job and it should be done quickly.
- If you are intending to show pupils' work, then ask each child to have their books out in individual piles with a name label, on chairs outside the classroom if possible. Make sure that the books are marked up to the previous day's date at the latest.
- If the meetings begin soon after the pupils leave, always make sure you have at least a short break for a cup of tea and a snack. An afternoon of teaching is thirsty work.
- You may feel more confident if you bring a change of clothes to school for the event. A discreet wash and change can make you feel fresher.

The Interviews

It is best to adopt a pleasant but professional manner. Be friendly but not familiar. Keep a discreet distance between you. The following might help.

- If it is your first time and you are anxious, try to get a support teacher to sit in the interviews with you, for the difficult parents at least.
  If you have a timetable of interviews, try to stick to it as closely as you can. Keep a watch or clock on the table if you can't see a wall clock. If a parent comes late, don't over-run to compensate.

It annoys the next parents on the list. If a parent comes very late, try to avoid letting them push in. Offer them another date. If you do over-run, apologize to the parent whom you have kept waiting.

- When parents come in, stand up to welcome them with a smile and offer your hand. Likewise, when they go, thank them for coming and any help or support they have offered.

- If they are known to be aggressive, take up a formal position behind your desk. Otherwise, sit facing them in the body of the classroom, on a chair the same height as theirs.

- Never have more than one set of parents in the room at a time, unless it is a large room and you can comfortably talk to parents without others overhearing.

- Make notes of any issues to be followed up as you go along, because it is difficult to remember it all after you have spoken to a long list of parents.

The vast majority of parents approach consultation evenings in a spirit of goodwill, but a small minority view it as an opportunity to air their grievances or try to catch the teacher out. I have known a small number of parents to admit that that is their purpose. Parents' questions can vary from the intellectual to the trivial.

Frequently asked questions and suggested answers

Q   How do you assess my child's capabilities?

A   Give a run-down of the tests which you use, e.g. reading and spelling tests, NFER tests, QCA or SATs GCSE tests, school's own examinations.

Q   How do you monitor progress?

A   I look at test (SATs, QCA etc) results and compare them to the previous year/term. Or

A   I look at the beginning of the exercise book and at the end and compare the two.

Q   Will my child be held back by less able pupils?

A   No, we always provide more stimulating work for the brighter pupils. Give details.

Q   What's your discipline like?

A   We try to maintain a peaceful atmosphere with a system of rewards and incentives. Explain the details.

Q   So far this term, a coat, a cap and a pair of gloves have been stolen from my child. What are you going to do about it?

A   Explain the lost property procedure. Emphasize that if the item is named, you do your best to return it to the correct person. If not, there is little you can do. Or

A   He has lost his homework book, a library book, a school pen and a CD. We'd like them back. Could you deal with this for us, please?

Q   Before my child came to this school, s/he was happy, lively and full of enthusiasm for learning. Since coming here s/he has lost interest and says that it's not worth getting out of bed for this school.

A   We were hoping you could tell us why s/he is so de-motivated. Or

A   Could it be hormones? Or

A   Has s/he made friends here?

Q   My child says s/he hates you because you are constantly blaming him for everything that goes wrong in the class. Why do you do it?

A   Because s/he normally is the one to blame. Or

A   I do blame others when they misbehave, but they usually accept a rebuke with a better grace.

Q   Our child is lovely with everyone except you. Don't you realize s/he hates your style and that's why s/he won't work for you?

A   I can please all pupils some of the time and some pupils all of the time, but not all of them all the time. Or

A   Pupils have to get used to lots of different teaching styles just as teachers have to cope with a wide variety of abilities and willingness to work in pupils. Or

A   It's a preparation for life, getting on with a wide variety of people.

Q   Our son doesn't mean to harm other pupils, he's just likes play fighting.

A   Fighting of every kind is forbidden because it often ends up with a pupil being hurt.

A   You would not like it if your child got hurt by a child who was 'play fighting'.

A   When he gets into a fight outside school, try using that excuse with the police and let me know their reply.

In most cases teachers and parents form a friendly, mutually supportive relationship but, unfortunately, it sometimes breaks down. The following are suggestions on how to handle a minority of problems.

Coping with aggressive parents

- Whatever happens, try to stay calm and in control.
- Occasionally, you can diffuse a situation with humour before it becomes nasty.
- Pass the buck, if you are young and inexperienced. Let the head of year or head of department cope with the hassle.
- If a difficult situation arises unexpectedly on parents' night, don't let it develop into a heated argument. It is better to make the suggestion, 'We need to discuss this more fully. Can you come back and discuss it when we have more time?' and make an appointment there and then. When they return for the next interview, make sure you have a senior member of staff present and have notes ready, as it can be difficult to think on your feet.
- It is often helpful to have a pupil's books ready in case you want to prove that the work is, or is not up to standard or shows a lack of care.
- If the parent is behaving in an intimidating manner or looking down their nose at you contemptuously, stare them out with an unblinking grin, as if you haven't noticed. It is difficult for them to keep it up if it is having no effect.
- For parents who raise their voices, start wagging their fingers, or banging their fists, say calmly but

firmly, 'I'm sorry Mrs Smith. I'm not prepared to discuss this while you are behaving in such an uncivil manner. Either you calm down and we discuss the matter like adults, or we will have to have this interview at a later date.' If they refuse to calm down or move, stand up and look at the door and say, 'It you would like to return and discuss this when you are calmer, that's fine. If they still refuse to calm down or leave, walk out.

- In extreme cases, write up your notes and pass them to your head or head of department.

- Never show any fear or dismay. If they turn up unexpectedly with daggers flying out of their eyes, stay calm and say, 'Oh Mr Bloggs, I'm so glad to see you. I was going to send for you.' Then start describing the child's latest misdemeanours.

- Make it clear you're not intimidated by threats. Counter, 'I'm going to the head,' with, 'That's fine. Off you go then,' and stand up, forcing them to either go or back down. If a complaint comes back to you from the head, make sure you point out that the complaint to higher authority was being used as a threat against you. Have all your facts ready.

- If you can, try to speak to the head before the parents do, because it also makes it easier for the head to deal with it if s/he know the facts in advance.

Violent parents

It is still rare for parents to physically assault teachers, but teachers' unions and associations confirm that it is on the increase.

- If parents are known to be violent towards their children, be careful to speak positively about their pupils to them. It is heart-breaking to discover that pupils have had an over harsh corporal punishment after you have informed the parents of their misbehaviour.

- If you have an appointment with a parent who is prone to violence, have a senior colleague, preferably the head, with you and try to keep a broad table between you.

- If a violent parent turns up unexpectedly, say, 'Can you wait a moment please,' and fetch the head or head of year. Never allow yourself to be alone with one of those.

- If a parent hits you, ask your union for advice and support fast. Take legal action. Your union or professional association should provide you with legal support. This is why it is foolish not to be in a union or a professional association.

How to cope with the whingers

In the past, some elements of the media and even some members of the government had negative attitudes to teachers and encouraged parents to question everything in their children's schools. Although this situation has improved, in the last twenty years, there is still a tiny minority of parents, who rarely express any appreciation and are permanently looking for an opportunity to complain.

These can be difficult because sometimes we have to face up to the fact that they may be right. You have to know your pupils and parents well to be able to differentiate between the parents with genuine complaints which must be taken seriously and acted upon positively, and those parents who complain regularly, as a matter of course and to whom you must stand up politely, but firmly.

It is wise to have answers ready.

If they complain that the work you are giving is too difficult, try, 'I am trying to stretch the pupils. They need to be stimulated to reach their full potential.'

If they say the homework is too much, a reasonable compromise might be, 'Let him/her spend 30/60 minutes on it, and I shall accept that even if it is incomplete.'

It they complain that the homework is too easy, try, 'Tracie never mentioned it, but if you're sure, I could set her some extra homework.' Or

'I don't mind trying her on harder work, but of course if she can't manage it, I shall have to put her back to what she is doing at the moment.' Or,

'The children have challenging work during the day and at the end of a long day in school they are usually tired. The purpose of the homework is to consolidate their work not necessarily to stretch them.'

It may be an opportunity to show work to the parents and tell them what s/he needs to achieve before you can give him something more difficult. Or, if exams are looming, it may be appropriate to say that you are revising to consolidate everything you have already done.

If they complain there is not enough homework, it may be worth mentioning that the pupils have worked hard all day and need a break to do other things to allow them to come back to school refreshed. You will need to justify this, so refer to any exam results, QCA results or class assessments to reassure the parent that their child is not being held back. Similarly, show them their child's books to reassure them they are achieving an acceptable level. If you are not actually giving homework, it is best to face up to the fact they are perhaps right and start setting it.

If they say their child is bored in your lessons, get out any attractive text books or apparatus you use to show them. Refer to any school trips or DVDs, which you have used to make the lessons more interesting. Describe how lessons are organized, because often parents do not realize how much trouble teachers take to make lessons enjoyable and stimulating. If you think they are more interested in complaining than the quality of education, I would suggest one of the following:-

'Perhaps you could explain to Ali that you only get out of your work what you put in. If he put in more effort instead of spending the lesson trying to worry the gerbil, he would get more satisfaction from it'

Or, 'I think it's rather fashionable to be bored at the moment. Most of the pupils in the class are quite interested in their work. I'm afraid it's down to Ali to put in the effort.'

If that fails, try, 'What do you do when he is bored at home?'

If they become really stroppy about it, as a last resort you could frown and say, 'If people are bored, it's their own fault, and they can do something about it. I'm never bored and I'm not sympathetic towards anyone who is.'

How to answer complaints about victimization – the 'You're always picking on my child' syndrome

Remember, occasionally they may be right because sometimes pupils irritate you so much, you find yourself inadvertently nagging them more often than the others.

Describe the child's behaviour quietly, in a purely factual manner. Explain how you have dealt with it and why. Involve the parents with comments like, 'If you can suggest a more effective way of dealing with it, I am willing to listen to you.' Show them that you respect their views and they can become supportive rather than confrontational. Try to give the impression that you like their child in spite of his/her misbehaviour. It sometimes easier to keep the parents on your side if you start positively. I often say, 'S/he's a good pupil in many ways but it is difficult to keep the pupils on task while s/he is calling across the room/disturbing the pupils who want to get on with their work etc.'

If they complain that you are victimizing their child by keeping him/her in at play time to work, point out that you are worried that s/he is slipping behind the others, because s/he wastes so much time in class. Again, describe how s/he avoids working and emphasize that you are anxious that s/he may slip down a set or have to go into a special needs group or end up with no GCSEs. Try to get across to them that your main worry is their child's progress and future success.

If the parents don't believe you, or still insist that you are victimizing their child, then you can turn it round and say, 'That's fine, next time s/he spends the morning faffing about, doing no work, I'll ignore it, but don't come complaining to me that s/he has made no progress at the end of the year.'

When they complain that your punishment for their child's hitting another child was too severe, just say, 'That's fine, next time a child punches your Jimmy, I'll be more lenient.' Give them details of how their child has inflicted pain on other pupils and ask them how they would respond if the same violence was inflicted on their own child. It is amazing how some parents have a different set of rules for how a teacher should deal with that issue, depending on whether it is their own or other people's children who do the punching and kicking.

Parents are rightly quick to complain, if their child is bullied. If there has been a complaint against the child, tell the parents about it but not the identity of the complainant, although they will probably find out from their own child. Parents are subject to peer group pressure as well as pupils, and knowing that other parents resent their child's behaviour frequently makes them back down.

The 'I know my rights' brigade

I find these people insufferable in any circumstances. The more they shout about their own and their children's rights, the less they care for anyone else's rights and the less responsibly they and their children behave.

When they complain that by sending their child out of the class for misbehaviour, you are depriving him of the education which s/he has a right to have, point out that keeping her/him in the classroom would be depriving the other pupils of the education which they had a right to have. Try 'I am expecting the other pupils' parents to complain about your child's disruptive behaviour and I intend to treat them sympathetically.' You may even have already had complaints. If so, tell them but never disclose which parents have complained. They will never trust you again if you do.

Generally when they launch into a speech about their child's rights say, 'You've taught him his rights, have you taught him to respect everyone else's rights? Have you taught him his responsibilities?'

When they assert that a child has no responsibilities, you can quite justifiably become teacherish and say something like, 'Of course they have. A child's responsibilities are to be kind to other children because they want other children to be kind to them. They have to respect other children's property because they don't want others stealing or breaking theirs. They have to obey the adult who is looking after them because no one can keep them safe otherwise. They have to tell the truth because no one wants or trusts a dishonest child, and they have to try hard with their school work to help them get on in life. If you get all that into children's heads by the age of five, they'll give you no trouble and you will be rewarded with the admiration and respect of other parents.' I've done it. Parents are so taken aback after listening to all that, they don't know what to say.

A very tiny minority, possibly because they suffered too much corporal punishment themselves as pupils, love to remind teachers and others that no one has any right to touch their child and if anyone ever lays a finger on him/her, they will sue for assault. If their child is fairly manageable, I should just smile and say, 'No problem,' and change the subject. If their child is prone to violent behaviour, look concerned and (if appropriate) remind them that now he is over ten, their child can be taken to court and sued for assault. If the child is under ten, remind them that if he continues to be violent, this will be the effect of his violence in later years. Remind them there are in Britain today, children as young as eleven in secure accommodation for crimes of extreme violence

Some of this might paint a dismal picture to a new

teacher, but remember that these cases are a small minority. In many schools, parents rarely present problems and are a constant source of help to teachers. Most parents are respectful, supportive, friendly and even grateful.

Although you must try to have a friendly working relationship with parents, you must make sure they treat you with respect. Never let them order you about. The rude, overbearing parents often back down or even give up when they realize you are not a push-over.

Don't feel too bad if you do cross swords with them, occasionally. I have never known a teacher who has ever achieved a peaceful relationship in every case.

3 And what are we here for? The pupils

Pupils can sniff out a weak teacher as s/he dawdles hesitantly through the doorway. If you stammer, avoid eye-contact, or speak in an over-ingratiating manner, you will immediately become a target of derision. Always keep your head up, your shoulders back, smile confidently, look them in the eye and speak as if you are taking it for granted that everyone will co-operate. Try not to look apologetic.

Your success with each class will depend on your relationship with them. Make sure you start on the right foot. Try never to lose your cool on the first lesson with any class, as it makes it horribly difficult to regain the pupils' trust. When they have become accustomed to your funny ways, it won't matter too much if you are lose it occasionally.

Teachers are usually nervous in their first week, so go to the loo just before you enter the classroom.

Building a positive working relationship

- In a secondary school, meet and greet the pupils at the door. This also ensures a punctual start to the lesson.

- In a secondary school where you have different classes of up to 30 a day, try to direct a question to each child, each lesson. It's difficult, but it helps to build up a positive relationship.
- At lunch-time, or in the corridor, nod or speak to pupils, as you pass. They appreciate being valued and aloofness leads to the breakdown of a relationship.
- Sarcasm is the lowest form of wit and the least effective form of persuasion! If it works at all, it is temporary and is counter-productive in the long run.
- If there is someone in the class whom you particularly like, try to hide it in case the 'teacher's pet' syndrome arises.
- Similarly if you dislike a child, hide it at all costs. Pupils, who know that they are disliked, love to create waves.
- With shy pupils, say a few encouraging words to them quietly as they leave at the end of the lesson.
- For future years, running after-school clubs helps to build up good relationships, but note that this is not a wise idea in your first year.

Motivating yourself and the pupils

The key to keeping pupils interested is being enthusiastic yourself. Pupils are quick to spot a lack of interest on the teacher's part. It is impossible to carry pupils along with you unless you can communicate the view that your lesson is worth having and of value to them. However you feel, crack on you are loving it. Use expressions like:

'This is what I enjoyed at school;'

'This is my favourite bit;'

'Last year's class loved this.' (They don't know this is your first year.) Use lots of incentives like:

'If you can all finish this, before the end of the session, we won't have any homework.' (Only use this one when you are not giving any homework anyway.)

'The table that's tidied up and ready first will go out to play first.'

'I know it's hard to concentrate on Friday afternoon, but if you can give me an hour of concentrated work, you can have the games out for the last half hour.' (Primary)

Primary pupils and even some secondary pupils love tangible rewards like stickers, certificates which you can run off the computer, ten minutes extra play for the whole class, if the head permits, even sweets but only if you are absolutely at the hair-tearing point. Never make the prize too attractive or expensive, because it raises the pupils' expectations.

Someone might accuse you of bribery and corruption in the case of the last two, but I should just smile and say, 'Nonsense! We all need a reward to work towards.' I would never use sweets in front of an inspector.

Dealing with questions and answers

Positive attitudes work best. It is so easy to point out mistakes and give negative instructions (no, that's wrong; don't do that) and so difficult to keep pupils interested after you have done it too many times. Often teachers are perplexed as to why pupils are so turned off, and are unaware that the teacher him/herself has actually disheartened them.

Put yourself in the child's place and imagine how you would feel if the only comments you got from your head/mentor were negative. Try these.

- When a child gives a correct answer, say,
  'Brilliant!'
  'That's clever of you!'
  'I can see you are good at this!'
  'You've obviously got a very mathematical/ scientific brain!'
- When a child gives an incorrect answer, try to give answers like
  'Nearly right,'
  'That's half right,'
  'A sensible/intelligent guess,' or
  'Keep trying, you're almost there.'
- When an answer is so far wrong you cannot say anything encouraging, say 'No,' gently and make a mental note to say something encouraging later in the lesson.
- When a child is difficult to engage in his/her work, start the lesson by asking an incredibly simple question and allowing him/her to answer. Then look delighted and say, 'Fabulous!' Repeat each time his/her attention wanders.

Organization – don't underestimate its importance!

Organization is vital. If you have forgotten some of your resources, you have given the pupils a delightful opportunity to play merry hell while you are distracted by having to rectify the situation. You also look as if you aren't sure what you are doing. Pupils are quick to deride a weak teacher and only respect and co-operate with teachers who look as if they are on the ball.

A few tips

- Always make extra worksheets because someone is bound to mess it up or a new child will join the class. Don't be too free with them otherwise the pupils think they should automatically have a new one each time they make a mistake.

- If worksheets are differentiated according to ability, have the ability group discreetly marked on the sheet. It's irritatingly simple to mix them up while you are simultaneously answering someone's question and sorting out misbehaviour.

- In your classroom, choose the notice board closest to your desk and pin onto it:
    your timetable;
    the names of the pupils in each group, or class in a secondary school;
    the week's literacy and numeracy plans (primary) and other weekly plans (primary and secondary);
    the sets of worksheets.

- Always keep spares of each exercise book ready for when pupils run out of space. If you don't, they might seize the opportunity to mess about while you send out for one.

- If you work in a school where there is a high turnover of pupils and you are given new pupils without notice, keep plenty of spare sets of books ready.

- Allocate each job to a pupil:- tidying up shelves with sets of exercise books, returning science apparatus to its correct place, books to the library etc. Remember that if a job is not assigned to someone it won't be done.
- Pupils like a rota system for allocating classroom jobs. They like the fairness of chores being shared evenly.
- If you use a lot of worksheets you can end up with thousands of pieces of paper. Have a system for storing them such as a folder for each child, keep the folders in alphabetical order and train the pupils to file their own work away.

Whatever happens, try always to keep the pupils on your side. This does not mean being soft and letting them away with misdemeanours. It means being organized, even-handed and letting them see that they are important to you. This brings us to the all-important issue of discipline.

4 The thorny issue of discipline Frequently called behavior management

Some teachers begin their career believing that they have an automatic right to each child's respect and co-operation, and in many schools it is a harsh lesson to learn that respect must be earned.

Class control can make or break a teacher. A fair to middling teacher with effective discipline can survive gracefully. An articulate and inventive teacher with brilliant ideas and poor discipline will have a hard time.

It takes a clever teacher to master the art of making sure that the pupils want to do everything the teacher's way.

Whole books have been written on behavior management. It is impossible to learn it all in theory, alone. You have to learn it by experience. The following should help you to avoid some of the difficulties.

Starting off on the right foot

Your ability to control each class is largely determined by the quality of your relationship with them. Try to keep it at the front of your mind that all pupils have a need to be considered worthy of your attention and care. If you can establish a relationship in which each individual pupil believes that you care for his/her well-being, this makes a firm foundation for a peaceful working relationship.

Discipline-wise, the first lesson you have with each class is the most important, because here is where you lay down the foundation for your future, working relationship. If you start off well, the rest falls into place more easily. If you and the pupils rub each other up the wrong way, it can take a long time to mend the situation. Most of the following can apply to either primary or secondary.

- Start each lesson on time; set the tone that they have to be present and prepared at the start of each lesson. This is especially important in secondary schools where pupils are changing class and have every opportunity to be late.
- Speak respectfully to pupils. Some teachers are quick with a cutting or belittling remark, which may work in the short term but stores up trouble for the future.
- When you acquire a new class, learn their names quickly. If you don't address pupils by their names when delivering an instruction or a rebuke, it's so easy for them to ignore you and pretend they thought you were talking to someone else. Name games help you to learn their names.
- Use a quiet, firm, polite manner to lay down your parameters before you start.

- Some teachers spend the first half-hour negotiating an agreed contract with the class, establishing ground rules of what teacher and pupil reasonably expect of each other, and pinning them up on the notice board. This works fine as long as the teacher sticks to his/her side of the agreement. For example, if the teacher agrees to mark the books each day/let the pupils out to play on time, and then does not keep it up, the contract falls apart easily.

- If you think you cannot cope with being consistent with a two-way contract you may find it easier to just lay down the rules and describe the consequences of them being ignored.

- Make it clear what you want pupils to bring to each lesson.

- If you know in advance that a pupil is likely to be tricky, it is a good idea to ask a teacher who has worked with him/her what works best.

- Also, catch him/her out doing the **right** thing. When they are doing what you want, say, 'That's cool, Simena,' It is so much more effective than rebuking them for doing the wrong thing.

- Establish a clear, simple routine to your lessons. It's not boring and humdrum: pupils like to know where they are and what's coming next.

- Always prepare more work than they can handle. The devil soon finds work for idle pupils.

The 'don't' list

- Never actually lose your temper. (I did it twice during my first term – once when I was told to 'go back to Ireland, you flippin' Irish git,' and once when I was kicked in the shins and told to go away, although the pupil did not actually use those words.) If you lose control of yourself, you cannot possibly control them. You can, of course, have a controlled loss of temper, i.e. just pretend to have lost it. It can work if you do it on rare occasions only.

- Never back pupils into a corner from which they cannot escape, otherwise they will come out fighting. Always try to give them an opportunity to get out of a tight corner and conform.

- Never trap yourself into an upward spiral of punishment, from which neither of you can escape. It leads to disaster. If punishment does not work after two or three attempts, try a different strategy.

- When pupils threaten to bring their parents to the school to sort you out on their behalf, don't look dismayed. Lift your diary and say, 'That's great, I was hoping to meet them, I'm free this afternoon, bring them in.' I have never known a parent to turn up after that.

- Try not to shout at pupils for misbehaviour. (Well, not any more than you have to.) Noisy teachers have noisy classes. It has more effect, the less often you do it.

- Never shout to attract attention from a noisy class.

- Never imagine that you know it all. I have taught for many years and am still learning new strategies. If you make mistakes, be prepared to learn from them.

The 'do' list

- Try to stick to the school behaviour policy as rigidly as you can.
- Be consistent. Pupils are quick to spot an inconsistency.
- Always give a clear explanation if there is a change of procedure. No one likes to be confused.
- Listen to pupils. They love it, especially the worst behaved. Often they don't have enough opportunity for conversation at home.
- Have a system for attracting everyone's attention. Some infant teachers rattle a tambourine. I always say, 'Hands up those who are listening and follow up by adding, 'Good, you can go out at break-time,' to those whose hands go up first.
- Another effective one is to release first, at the end of the session, the group who were all giving their attention first.
- In a secondary school saying, 'Quiet please, thank you. Quiet please, thank you. Third time, quiet please,' often works.
- Another strategy is to hold up five fingers and say, 'Five, four, three, two, one,' bringing down a finger with each number. Usually they are silent by the time you get to one.
- When a child is messing about when s/he should be working, start with, 'Can you manage? Would you like some help?' Not 'Stop talking/stop messing about/don't be so lazy.'
- When you get comments like, 'I'm not doing this, I don't want to,' smile sweetly and say, 'No

problem, you can do it at lunch-time.' Or 'That's fine. You can take it home and do it. I'll speak to your parents and tell them. They won't mind.' Whichever works best with the individual child. This often works, especially after you have carried it out a time or two.

- Remember pupils who don't respond to threats and sanctions often respond to praise. Use lots of it on disruptive pupils, when they are behaving well.

- Give positive instructions:- 'Please work quietly,' not, 'Stop talking,' or 'Write slowly and carefully to keep it neat.' Not, 'Stop rushing through it and making a scruffy mess.'

- Before imposing a sanction, give pupils a clear chance to conform. E.g. 'Your behaviour is not acceptable, you have got five minutes from now to get yourself back on track or your lunch-break will be spent in here working with me.'

- Be careful how you use the withdrawal of break-time sanction. It works well with some pupils, but others need that bit of space to unwind and withdrawing it actually makes their behaviour worse. If you do keep them in at playtime, always release them a few minutes before the end to go to the loo and get some fresh air.

- Always try to impose sanctions, the same day if at all possible. They lose their effectiveness if they drag into the next day.

- In one school where I worked, there was a system whereby pupils could earn a release from a sanction if they changed their behaviour and conformed. It sounds like letting them get away with it, but as long as their conforming to proper standards was substantial, it worked.

- Seating arrangements can alter pupils' behaviour. Seating boys beside girls sometimes calms either one of them down, or hard-working pupils beside those not so desperate to learn.
- Keep notes about any serious incidents in case there is any problem with parents later.
- Keep the praise flowing, but not so much that you devalue it.

Handling classes with disruptive pupils

If you find yourself facing a class with lots of problems, including poor behaviour often caused by poor teaching, poor parental support and a high turnover of teachers, you will need lots of positive strategies. Keep incentive schemes running. They work much better than constant threats and punishments. These are a few strategies which have worked well for many of my colleagues and me in the past.

All discipline strategies work with some pupils, and all pupils respond to some strategies. If something doesn't work, don't despair, because no one has ever got everything right first time. Just change the strategy.

The positive approach

Team points

I have known teachers to make disorderly classes work quietly by dividing their class up into four teams, each with a snazzy name, and putting a chart with each name on the wall and giving each team a point/sticker when they have worked quietly for a session, tidied up first, or all brought in their homework on time. The team with the most stickers at the end of the week gets a small prize. Always keep the prizes small or you end up broke. You can often find a pound shop or market stall where they sell packets of marbles, jars of bubbles, tennis balls and small novelties at four for a pound. This works well in a primary school.

In a secondary school, letting pupils off a homework is an attractive incentive but, of course, make it a revision homework so that they can't be left with a gap in their knowledge.

Merit boards or star charts

These are for individual good work, and are a good incentive. All the names are down the side of the chart and pupils are given stars or stickers opposite their name for good work or behaviour. You can give a prize like a chocolate orange at the end of the half-term. Make sure the stickers are for effort as well as quality of work, so that the slowest child in the class has as good a chance of winning as the most able.

Someone on the staff might disapprove because it is competitive. Smile calmly and say, 'But life is competitive. It will be good for them to learn to cope with it while they are young.'

Golden time

This is an effective strategy. Many schools use it as a basis for the whole school behaviour policy. The pupils are allotted twenty to thirty minutes at the end of Friday afternoon to do some enjoyable activity of their choice. If they misbehave during the week, they can have golden time taken from them in slots of one, two or five minutes. When the time arrives, they have to sit for the time withdrawn from them and watch everyone else enjoy themselves.

In some schools, pupils are allowed to earn their golden time back if they substantially improve their behaviour. This avoids the problem of some pupils, who have lost all their golden time by lunch-time on Monday, having no incentive to work and behave respectfully for the rest of the week.

Star of the day
At the end of the school day, the pupils are invited to nominate pupils who have shown most care and consideration for others/positive attitude/most effort with their work. The one with the most votes is named on the star of the day chart and next-day gets a reward e.g. a cushion for when they all sit on the carpet, the next day.

A special mention box
A shoe-box, covered in brightly coloured paper with a slot in the top and the words 'Special Mention Box' on a prominent label, is placed in an available position in the room. Pupils write down details of any kindness they have had from another child and put it in the box. They are all read out at the end of the week before golden time. It works because pupils love self-esteem and the child who writes the special mention often feels as good as the one who receives it.

Names in the jar
A colleague of mine used to keep a jam jar with a lid, and every time pupils showed an improvement in attitude,

effort, progress or care for others, their name was written down and put in the jar. At the end of the week the one pulled out at random got a reward. They soon realized that the more times their name went into the jar, the greater their chance of winning.

Marbles in the jar

This is a whole class strategy. If your class is habitually noisy, tell them there will be a marble in the jar for each fifteen minute working session, lining up and going to assembly, sitting quietly throughout assembly, where everyone, emphasize everyone, remains quiet. When the jar is full, everyone gets ten minutes extra play-time. You need the approval of the head for this one.

Sweets in the balance

An inventive colleague of mine brought a packet of sweets into school and took a weight balance out of the maths cupboard. He put a mass of 100 grammes into one side of the balance and every time a child showed improvement/effort etc, he ostentatiously put a sweet into the other. When the balance eventually tipped, the child who had earned the last sweet got all of the sweets in the balance.

That worked beautifully, especially when the pupils realized the balance was about to tip.

Fabulous fun trip at the end of term

For the horrendously difficult classes. You can only do this with the head's support.

Two of my colleagues told their ultra-challenging classes, there would be a strictly fun, non-educational trip at the end of term, for those who deserved it. A black dot chart was pinned to the notice board alongside the brightly coloured poster advertising the venue of the trip, and a nasty little black dot placed beside the name of each pupil each time they did not follow instructions promptly.

Those who had an unreasonable number of offending dots were left behind in school with work to do in another class, as the rest of the class lined up for a day's fun.

The improvement in attitude and behaviour was a delight to watch.

Each one of these works well with some classes, if they are carried out consistently. You can experiment and see what works well with each class. Obviously, if the pupils are well behaved and interested in their work, you don't need all these schemes.

Raising your pupils' self-esteem

Pupils with low self-esteem are more difficult to manage than those with high self-esteem. This is a strategy to raise pupils' feeling of self-worth.

Give each child a class list and ask them to circle their own name. Tell them to look at each name in turn, think about the child and write, beside their names, what they think is best about each one. Emphasize that it does not have to be their ability to cope with school work. They might be good at football, kind, honest, good at looking after their siblings or just good company. Tell them to write just one thing about each classmate.

Collect the sheets and type up, for each pupil, a sheet collating what everyone had written about them. Give each pupil their sheet of comments and time to read them. Tell them to put them into their school bags, take them home and keep them.

This is time consuming, but I know of a case where this was done and it had the effect of boosting the pupils' confidence and making them easier to manage. In later years, the teacher met some of the class and they told him how much the exercise had encouraged them.

Confrontations and avoiding them

Some teachers say, with some justification, if you get into a confrontation you have already lost. Some say you have only entirely lost if the pupil in the end does not bend to your wishes.

In either case you have certainly had your image tarnished, because the pupil has challenged your authority and probably caused amusement among his/her peers, gaining him/herself some kudos and embarrassment for you. Try to avoid confrontations at all costs, because they generate acrimony which frequently takes a long time to subside.

If you think one is about to arise, try to diffuse it with humour in the first instance. If that fails go up to him/her and speak quietly, giving two choices and describing the consequences in each case. That should give him/her an escape route.

If that fails, say, 'I can't waste time on this now, we have too much work to get through, we'll have to discuss it at lunch-time/break-time/end of the school day,' and keep a discreet distance between yourself and the pupil. If s/he continues to behave in a loutish or disruptive manner, say calmly, 'You are clearly not in a frame of mind to take part in this lesson, take five minutes out until you have calmed down and return when you are feeling better.'

It is best if during the five minutes out s/he is physically in the classroom. Warn the others not to interfere with the pupil, while s/he calms down. If the pupil calms down and joins in the lesson, never refer to the episode again. We all need our sins to be forgotten.

If a child storms out of the classroom in a temper, your reaction should depend on whether the school premises are secure, and the age of the pupil. There is no need to follow unless s/he is an infant or lower junior child in a building where the gate is unlocked during the day. In many schools, the gates are locked during the day. They usually come back if you ignore their exit. If s/he does not return by the end of the session, you will have to check up on her/his whereabouts, to ensure her/his safety.

At all costs avoid a screaming match, disruptive pupils love it and whatever the outcome, your image will suffer much more than theirs as a result.

If you know that someone is about to throw a tantrum, keep a few metres between him/her and yourself, smile and say, 'You can throw a tantrum if you like, give us all a laugh!' It often pre-empts it, but if it doesn't, make sure you do laugh.

Don't, under any circumstances, let any emotion other than amusement show. They won't be so eager to try it again if all they receive is ridicule.

Above all, never give in to a child who has thrown a tantrum. It is like throwing buns to crocodiles: they are bound to repeat the process for more.

Coping with the 'I'm going to wreck the class' mob

In many schools, pupils will conform if treated reasonably, but unfortunately there is sometimes a tiny minority who are determined to destroy the lesson, however much time you have put into making it interesting and enjoyable with an element of fun.
Try these strategies.

- If you have been warned that a pupil in your class is a right pain, make a point of saying something positive, to him/her in the first lesson. If they know you regard them as hell raisers, they will make a concerted effort to live up to your expectation.
- If a child tries to wind you up by passing wind in your lesson, ignore it and at the end, discreetly keep him (it is normally a boy) back and tell him you will be asking his parents to teach him a little anal control, if there is a recurrence. Never comment on the matter with other pupils around.
- Be strict about each detail with every class for the first term and by then you should have cracked it. In some schools you can only survive by keeping it up all year.
- If a child is disruptive, send for a parent early in the school year, before a problem grows too great. Approach the parent in a friendly manner, emphasizing that you are concerned about the child's progress. Ask if there is anything in school which might be upsetting her/him and throw in a comment about something s/he is good at. Then you can say that s/he has wrecked a variety of classes since the beginning of term and you are

concerned that he will not make progress, or other parents might complain.

- In a secondary school, make sure you and they know the sanctions and the chain of command - form teacher, head of year, senior teacher, for dealing with misbehaviour.
- Depriving a child of an activity which they enjoy – swimming, football – often works. In a secondary school you must clear this with the P.E. teacher first. Ignore the pupil's protests that s/he is entitled to those activities. Brush aside the retort, 'I have a right to…' with, 'It's not a right it's a privilege and you'll only get it if you deserve it.'
- When you hear the protest, 'That's not fair,' counter it with, 'It's perfectly fair because it's for your own good. You'll realize that in thirty years' time.'
- Only make realistic threats because once you have done it, you must carry it out. If you say you are keeping a pupil in at lunch time, you undermine yourself if you then relent.

Building bridges

- If, after a reprimand/sanction, the pupil conforms, lavish loads of praise and appreciation on him/her.
- Never bear a grudge. When the day is over, put it behind you and start the next day, as if the previous day's unpleasantness never took place. Pupils (and adults) appreciate that.

Rights again

The days of 'when in doubt, clout,' are long gone and today's pupils have more rights than the teachers, and they know it. It is usually the least respectful and most aggressive pupils who love to say, 'My mum says no one has any right to hit me. If any teacher ever lays a finger on me, my parents will take them to court and sue for assault.'

The answer is, 'That's right. No one has any right to hit you and you have no right to hit anyone else.'

If the pupil is occasionally violent and is already over ten, tell him that s/he can be taken to court for acts of violence as well, and remind him that in Britain there have already been children, as young as eleven, detained in secure accommodation, for acts of violence.

I used this line many years ago with a severely violent child, and was easily able to resist the urge to be sympathetic several years later, when I was informed that he had spent some time in one of Her Majesty's detention centres with expenses all paid.

If you can teach your pupils the glorious lesson that everyone else has exactly the same rights as themselves, you have done them a tremendous favour.

End of term syndrome

At the end of each term, try not to relax the pressure of work any sooner than you can help. Keep the pupils working as far into the last week as you can. Once you've dropped the work habit, you will not be able to restart it until the following term and the devil soon provides entertainment for pupils who are not occupied with something either enjoyable or worthwhile.

Some of this chapter might make you wary of working in a school where there is a lot of challenging behaviour. I have often found that in schools where there is a lot of challenging behaviour, teachers work together supportively and there is a happy atmosphere in the staffroom. If you find yourself in a school where there are difficulties with behaviour management, try to look at it positively. If you learn to cope and make a success of it, you will become a very confident teacher whom heads will want to employ.

5 Paperwork, planning and other time-consuming chores

Paperwork

One huge bugbear of any kind of teaching today is the copious amount of paperwork. In the Inset days before the pupils arrive in school, you will be approached by various senior staff who will treat you to a generous helping of written information.

When the head offers you the school handbook, look pleased and say, 'That looks interesting.' If the document is under 1 cm thick, (and this is not a joke) take it home and read it. These ones are usually well-written, tend to be succinct and contain most of the information you need to be going on with. If it is much thicker – some are up to several centimetres thick – put it on the shelf and refer to it when you need information. Never ask the head for information, until after you have consulted it first. If what you need is in the handbook, it irritates the head to know you have not read it.

In most schools there is a notice board in the staffroom and teachers usually have their own pigeon-hole and school email address. Through either one of these you will constantly receive flyers about courses, new books on the market, places for class visits, offers of people to come in to school to give educational workshops, updates on school policies, LEA policies, DfES policy documents, notification of oncoming school events and minutes of staff meetings. This is by no means a finite list.

You could not possibly respond to it all and still have time and energy to teach properly. The clever bit is knowing what must be taken on board or dealt with at once, what must be kept safe for later and what must be filed in the wastepaper bin (wpb) or scrap paper tray. I have a system whereby the urgent stuff goes on the notice board by my desk so that I can't lose or forget it. I keep a ring-binder marked 'Staff information' for all the school data and anything which might be useful later. Anything, which I'm sure I won't need, goes in the scrap paper tray or the wpb.

If you have a working area at home, it is worth photocopying the really important stuff, like the school holidays, to pin on your home notice board as well.

Being organized is vital. It saves you the irritation of wasting your precious time, three months later, searching for a flyer about a school workshop which looked useful. Also, other staff become annoyed with you if you lose some piece of school information which they have spent time typing up for your convenience.

Planning

In pre-national curriculum days, teachers used to draw up a loose plan for the term and work their way through it at the unpressurized pace that they considered suited the pupils' rates of learning and their own sanity.

In those lax, easy-going days, timetables were loosely

administered in a primary school and teachers did their lesson planning and preparation as the week progressed. Heads rarely asked for forecasts and record keeping was minimal. Compared with today's stringent practices, little was written down and when asked for a record of work done, the response, 'The work in the pupils' books is the only record you need,' sufficed. Frequently teachers decided what to do the previous day and sometimes while on the journey to work that day. (Them were the days!)

The curriculum was nothing like as regular or rigorous as it is today, but teachers suffered much less stress and the atmosphere in the classroom was frequently less tense and despite what some elements of the media would have you believe, the pupils did actually learn and enjoy it. In those golden days of teacher autonomy, the enormous freedom afforded to teachers gave an opportunity for their individual flair to shine out and inspire their pupils.

The requirements of the national curriculum and the accompanying forecast of medium term objectives, assessments, targets and evaluations have put several hours of labour per week onto the teachers' workload. Overseas teachers who are unaccustomed to it complain that having to write plans in such minute detail, leaves them with less energy to present the lessons with vigour and enthusiasm. However it must be acknowledged that better plans, on the whole, lead to more interesting and better organized lessons.

Remember your plans are your servants, not your masters. If during the week, you think of a better idea, don't be afraid to change the details.

A few tips to save time

- If the previous year's plans have not been handed to you, always ask for a copy of them. It's foolish to reinvent the wheel.

- If you work in a year group where there are parallel classes, split the planning into two or three, photocopy your lesson plans and worksheets and swap. It is time-economic for one person to run off the worksheets for the two or three classes for their area of planning because it is as easy to copy ninety as thirty. It also lessens the queue at the photocopier.

- The weekly plans usually have to be handed in on a certain day, each week. If you make it a priority to have them in on time, the head is more likely to have faith that you are doing everything properly. If the plans are often late s/he is more likely to keep checking up on you.

- Try discreetly to find out whether the plans are actually read them or not. A friend of mine asked the deputy head if he read the plans and got the reply, 'Read them? It takes me an hour to file them!' You can be less concerned about the detail if they are not read.

- In primary schools, for weekly literacy and numeracy plans, most planning is done on the computer. Some things are the same each week so if you superimpose each week's lesson on top of the previous or a similar week's plan you only need to amend the words.

- Keep a copy of every medium-term and weekly plan and work-sheet, all neatly organized in ring-binders with file dividers, or on computer files or disk, for each topic. At the end of your first year ask the head if you can stay in the same year-group, so that you can consolidate everything you have learnt this year. Another reason is, of course, so that you can re-use all your plans and at least save you hours of planning and preparation next year.

- Try to save time by using commercially produced worksheets where possible.
- Heads sometimes tell the staff that all planning and preparation are the property of the school and must not be removed from it. This is technically accurate but normally honoured in the breach. Most teachers, with an eye to the future, keep a copy of everything at home in the filing cabinet or at least stored on disk. You may be able to use it all in your next school.

Marking

Time-consuming and tedious as it can be, this is important and worthwhile because it is an integral part of the teaching process and unlike some paperwork tasks, it does actually benefit the pupils.

Most well-organized schools have a uniform policy for marking to make it easier for pupils to understand, if their work is marked by several teachers per week. If there is no whole-school policy you will have to organize your own and in either case make sure that the pupils understand it.

Make marking constructive for the pupils

For either primary or secondary. Put up a chart with an example of each mark and what it means. For example:

//	new paragraph
_____ (sp)	spelling error
( )	leave this bit out
√ (in the margin)	an interesting or clever expression/point to make
X(in the margin)	This bit is wrong.
_____ (gr)	grammar error
~~	This bit doesn't make sense.
N.R.	not relevant (secondary or upper primary)
N.A.	not applicable (secondary or upper primary)

When you give the work back, give the pupils a few minutes to look through it to see their mistakes and invite them to ask you if there is anything they don't understand.

You can make your marking helpful and encouraging with the following points.

- Use an erasable papermate. They are good for erasing your own comments when you want to change something in view of something you read later in the essay.

- Try not to mess the pupil's work up with great slashes of colour. A short deletion line is as effective as a long one and not nearly so disconcerting.

- Experts on dyslexia say that you should never use red or any bright glaring colour to mark the work of pupils with learning difficulties. This is understandable, since it is so disheartening if their work is returned covered with red marks. I always mark these pupils' books with a black pen or lead pencil with a much darker shade than the pupil's writing.

- If a piece of writing is completely riddled with errors, try to find an opportunity to take the pupil aside and ask him/her to read it to you. Write at least a few of the sentences out underneath for the child to see the correct version. It's clearer for him/her and not so depressing as masses of marks across his own work.

- Spelling corrections arise out of writing activities. Pupils with learning difficulties can only manage one or two at a time. Dyslexic pupils can manage one. The rest, up to a few per piece. Use your own judgment depending on the age group and what the child can manage.

- You don't need to correct every error in every

book. Gauge it to the individual child. If there are only a few errors per page, I mark them all. In the average book, mark several of the most obvious ones on each page.

- At the end of a writing lesson, give pupils time to confer with each other in pairs to look at each other's work and help each other to find their own and each other's mistakes.

- Write positive comments to encourage pupils to correct their weaknesses. For example, 'I like your ideas and choice of vocabulary, but try to concentrate on keeping it neat as well,' not 'This handwriting is dreadful,' even though it might be.

- Choose one thing and add a target for the next piece of writing, E.g.
  Target: Put a good ending onto your story.

Class marking

Take a piece of work done by a child and blow it up from A5 to A3. You can make this an acceptable practice by saying to the child first, 'You don't mind if I use yours, do you?'

Tell the class you have chosen this piece because you are so delighted with it and start by pointing out a few positive things about it, like neat handwriting or interesting vocabulary.

Invite the pupils to mark it one sentence at a time. Providing that this is done in a positive manner with constructive remarks, it should not cause embarrassment to the child. I have done it on a regular basis and found pupils were pleased when their work was chosen and it also helped pupils to learn to correct their own work.

Use stickers and stampers with words like 'excellent', 'terrific' and 'super work'. They save you time and even lower secondary pupils love them. If you teach modern languages, you can buy stickers with 'tres bien' and 'sehr gut' etc.

A few pointers to take the strain off you

If some work can be marked in class with pupils marking their own or another's book, then do so. Five minutes of class time can save you an hour of your own time. I always pre-empt pupils from cheating by saying the following, 'You could easily bump your score up by rubbing out any wrong answers, putting in the correct ones and pretending you got it right on your own. Is there anyone here who would be silly enough to do that? I shall not say a cross word to anyone who has every answer wrong, but I shall be disgusted with anyone whom I find cheating.' It doesn't seem worth the bother to cheat after that.

A few tips

- While the pupils are working at something which they cannot mark as a class, in unison, walk round the room and pick their books up, one at a time, and mark what they have done. This not only saves you time, but enables you to point out mistakes to pupils as they go along.
- If you are severely under pressure, during silent reading lessons, you can discreetly mark books while you have a confident reader beside you reading. It's not good practice so it is better not make a habit of it: only a last resort if you fear the

job is getting on top of you.

- Always collect books open at the right page, so that you don't waste precious time leafing through each book looking for the work.

- Try to mark at the most time-economic point in the day. Some teachers who commute, save time by marking on the bus or train. If you walk or drive to work it is often easier to mark in school where there are fewer distractions. If you have young children of your own, it is sometimes easier to take the books home, leaving school earlier to spend quality time with your own kids, and mark when they are in bed.

Everyday chores

Paperwork is not the only tedious chore. There are plenty of time-consuming tasks around the classroom. I like to cultivate the goodwill of the pupils who hate going out in the cold in the winter. They are usually willing to spend playtimes sharpening the pencils, tidying the book shelves, filing pupils' completed work sheets in their folders, cleaning whiteboards, taking work off the wall and cleaning out the hamster's cage.

If you do a lot of sports activities in secondary, it is worthwhile to select a reliable pupil to do the communication work of notifying team members about events, even if details are posted on information boards. This is a two-way benefit because responsibility teaches pupils reliability and gives them self-esteem. If a pupil becomes a regular supporter throughout the term, an end of term gift of a book token or similar is appropriate.

6   Taking assembly

Taking assembly in front of the whole school, or at least a substantial part of it, is a task that most teachers have to face eventually in their first year. In some schools, the list is put on the staffroom notice board with everyone's name written beside a date.

In primary schools, considerate heads do not normally force NQTs to face the ordeal in the first half-term, but you are less likely to avoid it in the second half. In secondary schools, where there is a larger number of teachers to share the rota, you may escape a little longer.

If the rota is blank for everyone to put their name after their chosen date, make sure you nip in fast and put your name at a date convenient to you. Otherwise you will be left with the space that no one wants, like the first week of term when you are bogged down with so many other new things to get used to, or the end of term when you are too tired to think about it, the pupils are restless and you have too many other things to do, like report writing and marking exam papers.

Each school has its own format for timing, organization and content. You will either have to take an assembly solo, or organize the class to do something entertaining or perhaps both. I find doing it solo easier because it takes about a tenth of the effort needed to organize and rehearse the pupils, but many teachers are so nervous about standing up in front of the whole school and staff, they always organize the class to provide the entertainment instead.

Even some very experienced, competent teachers who are so self-assured in other circumstances have told me they need to run to the loo a couple of times in the hour before it happens. I even had a colleague once who was so anxious she offered to do my playground duties for several weeks in return for my doing her assembly.

In your first year in any school, in the weeks leading up to your turn, it is wise to make a few mental notes about how your colleagues do it. Timing is important. You can discreetly time how long each teacher speaks or the class activity lasts. Heads don't like teachers to over-run or cut an assembly short. Note if the school has costumes or props, how to get them and the type of items presented. Some schools keep a record of each assembly and it is wise to look through it before you plan because it would be embarrassing if you duplicated one done recently.

School Policy on assemblies

You will also need to look at the school policy. Each LEA has an agreed syllabus for RE and collective worship in maintained schools. It must reflect the fact that the religious traditions of Great Britain are mainly Christian, while taking account of the teaching and practices of other principal religions.

Maintained schools must provide daily collective worship, usually through assembly, but in some schools this is honoured in the breach, unless there is an inspector present. Voluntary-aided and foundation schools with a religious character will determine their own policy.

The good news is that you do not have to worry about the school policy sticking strictly to the letter of the law because it is the head's responsibility. If s/he does not object to the content of your assemblies then you have no problem.

Some schools have a high percentage of ethnic minority pupils for whom mainly Christian based assemblies would be inappropriate. It is important to look closely at the school policy to see how the school deals with its multicultural aspect of assemblies, and then see how the policy is put into effect by watching your colleagues.

Don't be a shirker

It is unwise to try to opt out of taking assembly on religious grounds. It you take a secular assembly, it is unlikely that anyone will object. It you try to opt out completely, you would be viewed as lazy. If you find it nerve-wracking in your first year, ask your mentor for support, or another teacher with whom you have a harmonious working relationship, to do a joint one with you. Sometimes two classes join up and do two joint assemblies instead of one each.

Generally, if you admit you are anxious about something your colleagues will support you. If you try to shirk a responsibility their sympathy can dwindle.

Planning an interesting assembly

My best advice is read 'Assemblies Made Easy,' by V Kidwell (2004). It is a humorous book with lots of brilliant ideas, slickly written with pithy dialogue.

I am perhaps taking a liberty in suggesting my book, 'Class Assemblies for Primary Schools', available on Amazon. It gives thirty-six scripts for children to perform in assemblies. Each script has masses of parts so that they can be divided up fairly evenly among the children to avoid complaints from parents that their children have not had a big enough parts. There are scripts for each of the main religions and several secular topics.

Some schools have a theme which changes every half-term. I find these rather restrictive, but if your school has this policy there is very little you can do about it.

If you have a free hand, but are short of ideas, here's a few to try.

Religious festivals
Look at the current calendar for religious festivals.

As always, Google gets you everything. If you type 'calendar of religious festivals' into the search bar you will be spoilt for choice of multi-faith calendars.

Alternatively, if you just want information about one particular festival, you can of course Google it and get out plenty of information.

Saints' days
These can be fun. Even if you are not a religious person, lots of saints have an interesting story behind them and

pupils love to act, mime and tell stories in assembly. You can get information about each saint by googling them. Wikipaedia usually has some information on each saint and don't forget the good old-fashioned Children's Britannica and the Penguin Dictionary of Saints by Attwater et al. (1982)

Present a resumé of something you are studying in class.

For example, if you are studying the Victorian period, a short Victorian drama with a newsvendor shouting 'Read all about it!' followed by a documentary of a few important Victorian events mimed or dramatized by the pupils. It reinforces all your class work and the pupils love doing it: think of it as a revision activity.

An account of a school trip

Pupils love to present a resumé of outings. If you take photos on a digital camera and reproduce them on the screen, pupils are always pleased to tell everyone about something, especially if they are in the photos.

Look around your neighbourhood or within a few miles radius

Is there an interesting building with a history? Has someone well-known lived or worked there? Is there a park, museum or cathedral with an interesting story. Cities, especially London, are crammed full of interesting places. The closer to home, the more interesting the story will be.

Aesop's Fables

For Key Stage 1, these are a simple way to teach a lesson for life. Children love to tell, act out or mime a story and tell everyone the lesson to be learnt.

Use topical sporting events

These work well for key stages 2, 3 & 4 - the Olympic and Paralympic Games, the latest Marathon, the World Cup, Wimbledon. These are of premium interest to the pupils, especially secondary, and you can always find some moral or life skill to be held up as an example of good practice. Is there a performer who has demonstrated great courage and perseverance? Is team spirit an important issue? Has one of the team overcome some horrendous difficulty to succeed?

'Modern day' saints

There are plenty of people whose character, courage and devotion to others is exemplary – Mother Theresa, Gladys Aylward, Florence Nightingale, Mary Seacole, Nelson Mandela, Martin Luther King, Mahatma Gandhi, Maximilian Kolbe, Christopher Reeve.

Anniversary events, Jubilees, Independence days, Thanksgivings, National days – for example, Australia Day

For these, get out maps and show children where they are. You can always find plenty of details on www.google.com and www.yahoo.com. Tell the pupils how they came to be governed by a foreign power, how they achieved their independence and who were the people who brought it about. You can put together a PowerPoint presentation of the events.

'On this day, seventy years ago...'

In your local library there is probably a book telling about events which took place in the past on every date in the calendar. Or, of course, you can get it off the Internet. You are bound to find something interesting.

Use this idea carefully. It is much better to pick one interesting event and tell of it in detail, than just give pupils a list of events which you have found in a book or the Internet.

Who's your hero?
Jane Austen, Freddie Mercury, Walt Disney, Henry Ford, Thomas Edison, Charles Dickens, Mozart, David Beckham, Elvis, JK Rowling, Ellen MacArthur. Whoever you chose, each one is a fine example of something - talent, courage, perseverance, generosity, hard work, devotion to others, a determined pursuit for justice.

Key Stage 1 Birthday assemblies
These are held once per month with a mock cake and candles and are a fun event. Teachers and/or classes take it in turn to provide entertainment with a birthday theme. If you visit your local library, you will probably find lots of lovely story books with a birthday theme.

In the best one I've seen, a teacher put on an apron and prepared a cake with odd ingredients – vinegar, onions, mushy peas etc and sent it off with another teacher to be 'baked' while every sang 'Happy birthday' and a had a few pieces of light entertainment. The cake was then brought 'back from the oven' with pink icing and smarties for the birthday pupils to share.

Solo assemblies – a few hints
Preparation and rehearsal

- Practise it aloud and time it to make sure it fits the slot allowed.

- Whatever the topic, plan your opening line and questions, and interact with the pupils. I always start with a few simple questions. For example, if it were St Andrew's day, 'What date is it today?' 'What's special about today?' 'Put your hand up if you or your parents are Scottish?' This grabs their attention and distracts them from the conversation they were trying to have with their neighbours.

- Learn the script: never read unless you are nervous. It's so much easier to hold their attention with eye contact.

- If you cannot remember it all, write down about eight key words and hold it in your hand to discreetly use as an aide-memoire.

- Prepare a few visuals to keep the attention of pupils, particularly infants. PowerPoint displays work well. They look impressive and keep the pupils interested.

- If you are using a cassette tape or CD player, make sure you know where the power points are and use a reliable machine that you have used before. If using a tape, make sure it is all set ready at the right place.

- Plan a final line which finishes the story off well. Write it down if necessary.

On the day

- Make sure that you and your class are the first ones into the hall.

- Keep a glass of water handy.

- For background music, play something pleasant

but soothing, not loud or lively because it makes it harder to settle them down.

- If you feel at any time you are losing their attention, ask a few more questions to get it back.
- Fix your eye on a child and make eye-contact and then slowly move your eyes around so pupils feel you are addressing them personally.
- A bit of play acting helps to keep their attention. Put on different voices for different characters, mime a few of the actions while narrating and exaggerate your facial expressions.
- Don't forget the music on the way out.

Class Assemblies – why they are worth the extra work

These are time-consuming to prepare but well worth the bother. Pupils love people to listen to them, and it gives an opportunity to shine to pupils who do not have much chance to shine in class. I always try to give the less able pupils as prominent a part as they can handle. Pupils who are attention-seeking in class often thrive in front of an audience.

Pupils can be nervous beforehand but overcoming it is just part of the process of growing up. Performing in front of an audience is an invaluable part of their education because it builds up their confidence and self-esteem. In schools where there are regular class assemblies, the practice often enhances the quality of end of year productions and Christmas concerts.

Planning

- There must be an element of fun, so the pupils will want to perform and so that the audience will enjoy listening. Try to throw in a few jokes.
- The assembly should have an objective: a lesson to be learnt.
- The lesson does not have to be something with a high moral tone. For example, on the third week of April, the objective may be to awaken the pupils' interest in the life and works of William Shakespeare.
- If you have an objective of the last type, you could add the moral that if you have a talent, you should use it to enrich your own and everyone else's life; or if you want to do something exciting with your life, work for it, reach for dreams, aim for the sky. There's always something.

Practising

- Pay special attention to clear speech which can be heard at the back of the hall. Teach pupils to lower the pitch of their voice to raise the volume and to speak more slowly. For the first practice, I sit at the back of the hall, and say, 'I can't hear you,' whether I can or not.
- It helps to share the workload. If you want them to sing a song, ask the music teacher. If you want them to do a dance, ask the PE teacher. Specialist teachers are usually helpful about letting the pupils practise during PE and music lessons or at least playing the music onto tape for you to use to practise or showing you how to organize a dance.
- If you are using a long poem or a story, try to split

it up into as many parts as you can, even if you have twenty narrators with a few lines each. It means everyone gets a turn and no one has too many lines to learn.

- As with solo assemblies, try to make sure everyone memorizes their part. Reading it never has the same effect.

On the day

- Pupils in Key Stage 2 often want to dress up for assembly. This could lead to hours of extra unnecessary work. If there is a school costume cupboard, fine. Otherwise tell the pupils that costumes don't matter but if they want one, they must provide it themselves.
- Emphasize that it is the quality of performance which really counts, not the costumes.
- As with solo assemblies, don't forget the music for entry and going out.
- At the end of the performance, publicly thank any of the staff who assisted you.

When it is over

- Mentally evaluate. I always judge the quality by how well the audience sits still and listens. Make a note of anything which might be helpful for the future.
- After you have stopped sighing with relief, lavish lots of praise, house points and stars etc on the class afterwards.
- If someone has made a mess of something it is best just to laugh and tell the child it doesn't matter. My stock line is, 'Don't worry Freddie, I

have made much bigger bloomers than that.'

- Keep a record of every assembly you do. I have a file with all my scripts, overhead projector acetates, and notes retrieved from the Internet. Keep your PowerPoint displays on a memory stick. This is not another useless piece of paperwork. You can use them in your next school or in the same school if you wait for about four or five years.
- If another member of staff has had a large input, a box of chocolates or a bottle of wine is appropriate to show your appreciation.

Assemblies are like everything else, the more you put into them, the more you will get out of them. If the rehearsals are fun and you give pupils the opportunity to build up their confidence and self-esteem, you will also be improving your relationship with them and increasing their allegiance to you.

7 Organizing day trips

School trips. Why bother? There has been much controversy surrounding school trips in recent years. Each year in British schools, hundreds of thousands of pupils go on school day trips and return to their parents safely and happily having benefitted from the experience. Unfortunately a small number have resulted in minor accidents and in a few extreme cases, tragedy generating understandable grief and anger on the part of sadly bereaved parents.

Some teachers who have successfully undertaken trips for years are now anxious at the prospect of facing parents if the worst happens, or the shame and strain of court proceedings if an accident takes place and charges are pressed.

Litigation is becoming a popular trend of our society, with numerous companies touting for business with slogans about blame and claim. This makes teachers feel that they are in vulnerable positions. Some unions have advised their members against undertaking school trips for fear of being sued if an accident happens. This may be an understandable reaction, but I fear it is an over-reaction.

Every day in life, someone is killed in a car accident, but that does not stop anyone from going on a car journey. If we all take the view that we must not undertake trips, then we end up with the situation, where no one does anything extra to enhance pupils' experiences, and education becomes a bland, less exciting and stimulating experience.

I have always enjoyed school trips and thought them well worth the extra work. The advantages are manifold.

- They are usually great fun and a break from the routine of the classroom.
- They provide pupils with hands on experience which reinforces your lessons and transforms theory into reality. For example, a trip to Butser Ancient Celtic Farm brings the Celtic period to life. A trip to a Shakespeare play or film inspires the pupils who were not inspired by the black print on the page.
- In the follow-up lessons in school in the days which follow, the quality of pupils' work always shoots up.
- It is an effective bonding experience. Your pupils' allegiance towards you increases when you give them an exciting day out.
- Pupils are so pleased that you have taken them out that they usually behave better on trips.
- School trips awaken pupils' curiosity about the world and increase their urge to find out more.
- They can be used as rewards for good behaviour and, in rare occasions only, exclusion for bad.

A few drawbacks

While I am such a keen believer in the value of school trips, I have to report, with regret, that there is a downside.

- Contrary to the opinions of some outside the profession, they are much more tiring than a normal day's work.
- They involve an extra load of tedious paperwork – risk assessments, insurance rules, letters to parents and collecting their permission slips and money.
- The dangers are bound to increase when you take pupils through the gate and on to the road, and you are responsible for their safety.

Planning the trip

You are unlikely to have to take overall responsibility for planning a trip in your first year, but you will probably have to assist with one.

For the future, when you are planning a trip always visit the venue's website in advance. In the week or two before the trip you can often use it to plan an ICT lesson or devise one in conjunction with the ICT teacher. For example you could give the pupils a list of things to find out from the website of the venue or ask them, in groups, to write down a list of things they want to find out on the trip. Ask them to think up questions about the venue.

You also need to visit the actual site, even if it is quite far away. If it is very far away, your school should help you with travel in the form of a train fare or petrol allowance, although you may have to visit it in your own time.

Use this as a checklist to find out what you need.

1   The opening and closing times
2   The entrance cost including all the adults. Some places allow teachers in free if you explain that you are coming with a view to bringing your class there and some allow all accompanying adults in free on the day of the trip. Some add the condition that free entrance is in return for keeping the pupils quiet and well behaved.
3   The location of all the toilets
4   All of the facilities and educational activities which are available to schools, their costs and how much notice must be given to book them.
5   Is there a room for the pupils to eat their packed lunch? If not, try to find somewhere suitable.
6   The gift shop. Look at the prices and estimate how much money you think is sensible for the pupils to bring. If it is overpriced, it is best to exclude it from the trip. You also need to find out if there are rules about how many pupils they allow in at once.
7   Plan work for the pupils to do, or things for them to find out while they are there if it is appropriate. Some museums and cathedrals provide worksheets. Check if they are pitched at the right level for your class. You may need to prepare your own. It is tempting to buy one of the venue's sheets and photocopy it. This is mean because they make so little money out of them, and it could be embarrassing if they catch you breaking

their copyright.

8   The location's safety policy. You may need to sign an agreement to abide by it.

9   Decide the mode of transport. If booking a coach it must be done well in advance.

The letter to parents

Even at secondary level, pupils can only be taken on trips with parents' written permission. You must write a letter to parents giving the following information.

The date and location

One sentence explaining the objective, e.g. 'to consolidate their topic on the Romans in Britain'

The mode of transport

The cost. In state schools you must say that it is voluntary and no child will be excluded for non-payment.

The times of leaving and returning to school

Ask the parents to make sure their pupils bring any of the following which are necessary:-

1   packed lunch – no glass or nuts, other pupils may be allergic;

2   waterproof jacket or mackintosh;

3   polythene carrier bag to sit on if you will be eating out of doors;

4   pocket money - a modest and specified amount, in a named purse or wallet;

5   something to amuse themselves on the journey if it is a long one, and confirming that each pupil must be responsible for its safety;

6   medication e.g. asthma inhalers, pills in a named container to be given to the First Aider;

7   sensible footwear – trainers, wellingtons, change of socks.

Ask the parents to sign the permission slip attached to the letter and state whether their son/daughter may return home alone after the trip, if it is after the normal home time. Always remind them that pupils cannot be taken on a trip without the written permission and set a deadline which is about a fortnight in advance of when you really need it.

In a state school, if parents are unable to pay, the school must accept the cost, but if the permission slips are not signed and returned then, sadly, the pupils must be excluded. I have known this to happen and it causes pupils understandable grief, as well as giving the teacher the extra chore of setting work which the pupils can do without support, and finding another teacher to have the pupils in his/her class for the day. That is why it is best to leave yourself plenty of extra time to chase up the parents who consistently forget about it.

Paperwork

There are, of course, a few common sense precautions.

1   Read your school policy on school trips and as long as you make sure you stick to the letter of it, especially the safety precautions, you cannot be blamed if anything goes wrong.

2   Take more adult helpers than the school policy demands – classroom assistants, part-time staff,

parents or governors. The cost does not matter: safety does.

3   Check the insurance. If you are taking parents or people who are not members of staff, they may have to sign something to include them on the school's insurance for the day. Check with your mentor/headteacher/environmental studies co-ordinator.

4   Fill in the school's risk assessment questionnaire. It is best to do it well in advance because there may be a section to be filled in by the venue's administrator and so that you have time to organize anything extra which the head asks of you.

Adult Helpers

- Choose your parent and governor volunteers helpers carefully. I find the best parent-helpers are the ex–teachers because they know how much responsibility they must take on and do not imagine that the day out is a relaxing treat for them.

- Remember, parents need to be checked out by the Criminal Records Bureau (CRB) just as teachers and other school staff. Some schools keep a register of willing parents who have been checked out by the police for the purpose.

- Always give parents, who are not being paid for their day's work, an easy group of well-behaved pupils.

- If bringing a parent, who has never been on a school trip before, always explain any safety procedures and emphasize that the pupils cannot be left unattended at all. I know a parent who nipped off to a café for a cup of tea and a sandwich, during a trip.

- Give each adult helper a pack containing the timetable and organization for the day, the class groups and their leaders, each leader's mobile phone number, pens or pencils, information about the venue and copies of the work the pupils do during the day.

The Pupils

Always make the following points clear.

- Only those who can behave perfectly will be going. This is an absolutely reasonable request. Remember that pupils, especially teenagers, like to push the boundaries out. If you want excellent behaviour, demand perfection.

- Anyone who lets the side down will be excluded from any further trips and **make sure you carry it out**. Failure to do so undermines your discipline for the future and antagonizes the pupils who have made the effort and had their day spoilt by the misbehaviour of others.

- Serious misbehaviour will result in their being immediately escorted back to school. This is another reason for having extra adults. Unfortunately you can only say this if it is practical for you to carry it out. You look weak if you make the threat and then don't follow it through.

Beware of ever believing that anything is 100% safe because that leads to complacency and becomes a potential danger.

Using public transport

This is the cheapest but unfortunately the most problematical to organize. Secondary pupils are usually mature enough to be trusted to behave responsibly on buses or trains. In some cases, secondary pupils over sixteen can make their own way to the venue, with written permission from their parents. I once worked in a special school where finding their way safely to the venue and back was part of the syllabus for citizenship.

Primary age pupils need reminders about behaviour and safety before you leave and lots of supervision en route. The following tips might make it run smoothly.

Safety

- When you cross a road, always have an adult on the road to supervise if the pupils are walking in a crocodile.
- Use pedestrian crossings and pelican lights on busy city roads if you can, even if it means walking further.
- Some LEAs have a rule that pupils must line up on the kerb and everyone crosses together. This minimizes the time taken for everyone to cross.
- Count the heads twice before you go and every time you get off or on a bus or train.
- Designate one adult to be the last on and last off

the bus or train. This ensures that you do not leave anyone behind.

- Warn the pupils that if they do get left behind on a bus or train, to go to the next station/bus stop, get off and wait on the platform or kerb until an adult come for them. This is another reason to have extra adult helpers. You should miss them straight away if you count the heads as you get off the bus or train.

Organization

- Find out who in the class becomes travel sick. Ask their parents to give their children travel sickness pills before they leave home and ask them to send one in to the First Aider for the journey back.
- Divide and rule. Allocate a written list of a small group to each adult to supervise and regularly count as well. It's easier for each adult to count six or seven than to rely on yourself to count thirty or more.
- Always put the pupils with medication into the First Aider's group.
- If you work in a city school, never travel in the rush hour. I used to wait outside the tube station with the class until a minute after the deadline time. It is also cheaper then, as well as more comfortable.
- Where possible, buy the tickets in advance. It saves queuing and avoids pupils becoming restless while waiting.

What do you bring with you?

Personnel

- More helpers than the school policy demands
- A member of staff who has completed a First Aid course. It is worth doing the course yourself. It's four days off school and has to be renewed every three years. It's useful because you don't have to go looking for a First Aider every time you want to go on a trip.
- An adult who doesn't mind cleaning up after a child has been sick.

Equipment

- The First Aid kit and pupils' medication. This is usually carried by the First Aider or teacher with the relevant pupil in his/her group.
- Sick bags, rubber gloves, bottle of disinfectant, tissues, a few old newspapers to wrap up the sick bags before discarding them and a bottle of water. Never underestimate their importance.
- A cheap old perfume. If a child is sick, spray it over the vomit to kill the smell so that it won't make you or anyone else sick, before it is cleaned up.
- A list of all the pupils' names and parents' home telephone and mobile numbers, in case a child falls ill or has an accident and needs to be rushed to hospital.
- A few extra vegetarian sandwiches. There is usually someone who forgets their packed lunch

and hungry pupils are more bother in the afternoon.

- Extra money, in case something unforeseen happens and you need to pay for a taxi, suntan lotion, anything.
- Clipboards and pens/pencils, sharpeners, rubbers, sharpeners, worksheets.
- Drinks, and even biscuits perhaps, for the end of the journey if it is a long one.
- A digital camera, so you can run off dozens of pictures. Pupils are always more keen to write about something if they have a photo of themselves beside it. They also like to keep the picture to illustrate their work, or as a souvenir of the day.
- Optional - a camcorder. Putting events of the day on the smart-board jogs pupils' memories when they do the follow-up work.
- Black bin liners to clear up all the mess after the packed lunch.
- Make sure each helper has their mobile phone.
- Sanitary towels, if taking girls in year 5 upwards.

Travelling on a hired coach

This is usually expensive but much safer and simpler.

- Check beforehand that there are seat belts and make sure everyone is belted up before you move off.
- If a pupil refuses, have him/her excluded from the trip. If a pupil refuses to belt up on the way

home and it is too late to exclude him/her from the trip, sit beside the little gem with your hand clamped over the inserted belt buckle and ignore all the protestations about your having no right to infringe his freedom of movement. (I have done it twice.)

- When you return to school, tell his parents that you have no choice but to exclude the pupil from the next trip. When they object, point out that it is for his own safety. Do not back down.
- Make sure the windows are shut and the coach air-conditioning is on. If the driver is unhelpful, tell him that it stops the pupils from being sick. They never argue after that.
- If the coach has no air conditioning, open every window. Explain the advantages of avoiding food regurgitation if the driver objects.
- When you return, ask one of the helpers on the coach to scout around and check that everything has been removed from it. It can save you time contacting coach companies to retrieve items left behind.

When you return

Personnel
- If the head agrees, tip the coach driver, if s/he has been helpful. Your school may need to use the company again.
- Stay with the pupils until the last one has been collected, unless they are old enough to go home alone.

- Personally thank each individual helper. It is vital to keep their goodwill because you are bound to need them again. Sometimes, it is appropriate to invite them into the staffroom for a cup of tea, or your classroom if there is a policy not to have parents in the staffroom.
- As a courtesy, let the head know that everyone is back safely.

Equipment

- Grab all the clipboards and worksheets. The pupils will be too excited to remember them.
- Download the photos from the digital camera or ask the ICT teacher or a smart pupil to do it for you. Put them into a folder on the desktop so that they are accessible to the children.
- Email a note of thanks to anyone at the venue who has been helpful.

Suggested follow up work

Of course it depends on the age of the pupils and this is by no means a finite list.

- Ask each group of pupils to write or type a letter of thanks to their group leader, telling them what they enjoyed most about the day and to anyone at the venue who made it an enjoyable day. This can be done by email. The pupils prefer it and it's just as effective.
- Make a class book or large display about the day. Include pupils' own drawings, downloaded

photos or even pictures cut out of leaflets or from the Internet.

- Make their own individual books or poster about the day, using resources suggested in the last point. Pupils prefer these because they can take it home as a souvenir afterwards.

- Ask the pupils to write down questions about the trip. Make a list and ask the pupils, in groups, to find the answers using the Internet, encyclopaedias, reference books. Have a session of reporting back to the class. Pupils often love this because it gives them the chance to play the part of the teacher.

- Use the day as a basis for your next class assembly. It saves you having to think up an idea and it reinforces what the pupils have learnt. If you plan this in advance it is worth having digital photos on PowerPoint to illustrate it.

All of this might make day trips sound time-consuming and tedious. Fortunately, you will be broken in gently as someone more senior will do the organizing for you in your induction year. In later years, you will become accustomed to the procedures and hopefully have the pleasure of seeing how your effort has enhanced the quality of education for your pupils and improved their attitude and standard of work.

8   Report writing

Writing reports is an important task which takes up many hours of your time each year.

It is better not to begin with a brief outline of what the class has studied during the term before typing anything about the child. I know one school which was heavily criticized by Ofsted for doing so, because the report is meant to be exclusively about the child's progress.

In most schools, the reports are set up for the teachers to type online. Many teachers make the task easier by typing a report, then copying and pasting it onto similar children's report. It is very important to read the first one a few times before you start copying and pasting it, because if you make a mistake you have to correct it on every report. Look carefully at your comments with the pupil in mind. You will need to edit the details to make it appropriate for the individual. If you have twins in your class, make sure their reports are not absolutely identical, because this understandably irritates the parents.

Try not to cut and paste anything that has a child's name on it, because you might inadvertently send it out with the wrong name. It annoys the parents and is very embarrassing when they complain.

It is best to type all of one gender first to avoid having to keep changing the pronouns and possessive adjectives. Parents complain if reports refer to their daughter as 'he' or 'him'.

Try to avoid using the words 'good', 'well', 'bad', and 'badly'. They are boring words and you can usually find a more descriptive one. Your report writing will look and sound much more professional if you use interesting, thoughtful expressions, like the ones below.

Proofreading your own typing is difficult because you tend to read what you think is there. It is worthwhile to team up with a colleague and proofread each other's reports.

Positive comments which parents like to read

- contributes sensibly;
- shows clear understanding;
- takes pride in;
- listens attentively;
- likes to take part in;
- lively imagination;
- sound general knowledge;
- has a wide range of interests;
- always tries his best;
- is quick to take in new information;
- has an efficient memory for;
- is well organized/fluent/responsible/enthusiastic;
- sensible/careful worker/continues to improve;
- retains facts easily;
- able to grasp concepts easily;
- applies him/herself sensibly to all areas of the curriculum;
- joins in all activities enthusiastically;
- enjoys lessons; and
- continues to progress and develop.

The word 'average' is currently out of vogue and many teachers react - I sometimes think overreact - to it. I think these are better:
- works well with the middle range of the class;
- can keep up with at least half of the class;
- can work independently, although s/he does not rise to the top of the class.

Negative comments which parents can accept more readily

It is much easier to write a positive report than a negative one. Parents are often upset by negative comments. In some cases it can cause embarrassing arguments and I have even known cases where parents have wanted comments removed and reports rewritten.

Tact is absolutely necessary to tell the truth and still keep the parents' support and goodwill. These phrases are designed to tell the truth without causing offence.

For the less able
- slow but steady;
- tries hard but has difficulty with;
- puts in great effort but lacks confidence/concentration;
- puts in effort but needs a lot of support and encouragement;
- needs lots of practice at each level;
- copes best in a small group; and
- needs extra practice in basic skills.

For the unenthusiastic
- his inability to concentrate is having an adverse effect on his own progress and that of others;
- sometimes makes avoidable mistakes;
- needs to take more care with;
- needs to be treated firmly to stay on task;
- needs to put in more effort to keep up with the group; and
- often needs to finish off his work at break-times.

For the child with poor social skills
- has some difficulty in making and keeping friends;
- does not yet understand how his behaviour affects other pupils' reactions to him;
- does not always respect other pupils' space; and
- must learn that a glib answer or giving back-chat will not get him what he wants.

This website is useful. www.reportwritingbank.co.uk

It is never wise to write anything terribly pernicious on a report, however much you feel it may be true or justifiable. Remember these reports stay in a file for years and it hardly seems fair that someone should be reading something awful about a child several years later. Some say that reports should be written on paper which self-destructs after about five years. I'm inclined to agree with that.

If there is anything very unpleasant to tell, I always say to the parents on consultation evening, 'I haven't written this down for people in the future to pick up and read. I prefer to just tell parents quietly in private that ...' Put like that, parents are more likely to accept it and they appreciate a teacher's keeping their child's worst attributes private.

Getting the tone right as well as getting the information across accurately is the most important part. If this is your first year or you are new to the school, do not worry about having a reaction from the parents, because all reports are ultimately the responsibility of the head. After you have written them, the head must read and sign each one. That signature represents his/her approval, so if there are any objections from parents, the head must support you.

Report writing is very time-consuming and tedious and unfortunately often has to be done in the latter half of each term when teachers are more tired or already encumbered with other tasks like marking exam papers. As soon as you receive your report sheets or disks, it is wise to start them straight away. I like to work out how many I should do per night to finish with a week to spare. Those teachers, who leave it to the last minute, end up working until two in the morning and giving a poor performance in class or irritating their colleagues by taking a sickie when everyone knows why.

Be kind to yourself. When you have finished, reward yourself with a night out, or, if you have children of your own, take them on some non-educational trip to compensate them for neglecting them while you have been struggling through all the extra typing.

9 The politics of the staffroom
Who's your friend?

The politics of the staff room can be an unholy business. I have known one mature person who, after doing her pre-course placement in a primary school where the atmosphere was particularly unpleasant, decided to withdraw from a PGCE course, and an experienced teacher who resigned and took three part-time jobs to avoid it. You can preserve your sanity and survive more gracefully by staying out of staffroom politics as long as you can.

The staff are like the head's class. An even-handed, kindly, efficient teacher usually has a happy, united, hard-working class and the same applies to the head and the staff. There are many excellent heads who can take a widely differing group of teachers and mould them into a happy, united, effective team. If you are fortunate to be in a school like this, then you do not need the advice in this chapter.

Factions in the staffroom

When the staffroom has factions in it, not only do the pupils sense it, exploit the situation by getting through the cracks, but the more aggressive and power-happy teachers do so as well. Strong heads keep a staff united by their own even-handedness and refusal to give ears to any teacher criticising or complaining about another. Some weak heads feel threatened by a united staff and consciously or unconsciously set about creating divisions.

I have known schools, where the staff could be divided into two or three groups:- those in favour with the hierarchy, those not, and those who are ignored by the hierarchy.

If you are in a school with factions, it is important to keep quiet at least until you have worked out who is in each clique. Even then, it is still usually best to stay out of all of them. This ensures you have no enemies but it may also mean that you have no close friends on the staff. Staffrooms can be divided in lots of issues like:-

those who support the head and those who don't;
those who want the school to use more modern techniques and those who prefer a traditional approach to everything; and
those who encourage more parent power and those who like to marginalize the parents.

Whatever the issue that divides the staff, it is best never to comment on it at all, in your first year. Nor is it wise to try steering a mid-path between two factions who want to move in opposite directions. People who walk up the middle of a road get knocked down by cars going in both directions.

Staffroom sneaks

Even in your second year it is sensible not to comment

negatively on anything in the school unless in private and you are certain you can trust the person to whom you are speaking. Some heads have a super-grass – a teacher who sits in the staff room quietly listening in to everyone's conversation and then reporting it back to the head. To test out a suspected super-grass, I used to pick up the TES and comment to her about available jobs. After two such occasions, I was summoned to the office and asked if I was looking for a new job.

It is safest to listen quietly to people who moan to you, but don't enter into the conversation until you know whom you can trust not to repeat your comments, and who likes running to the head to drop teachers in it. There is nothing worse than telling one of your peers what you dislike about the head and then discovering that s/he is having an affair with him/her.

Some teachers watch their colleagues and report them to the head for any misdemeanors – losing/breaking a piece of equipment, coming in late. Some say one thing when the head is present and the opposite when s/he is not. Beware of the deputy heads who criticize the head negatively. They usually run the staff down to the head as well.

If you have any of the above in your school, it is better to stay well away from all of them. Sometimes young teachers are tempted to cultivate their friendship as they are seen as safe company. Any friendship which these teachers offer is superficial, can be withdrawn at any time, and frequently is.

The doom and gloom lot

A minute number of teachers have poor attitudes and are

constantly moaning. Worse, they generate a negative attitude which can grow and spoil a happy atmosphere. It is best to smile, say, 'Good morning,' and move on. Keeping your morale up is vital to being able to enthuse pupils and stay on top of the job, and these people can depress you.

Getting personal

At the end of term staff party, it is sensible to avoid anyone who has any power, and avoid the sickening feeling of waking up the next morning and remembering what you said while under the influence.

Occasionally, heads and deputies conduct romantic liaisons with members of staff. You can suss it out by the extra confident swagger they suddenly acquire, or the over-zealous manner in which one defends the other when they are challenged. This causes consternation among the staff, because great powershifts ensue. It causes no problem if one of them leaves, or they at least conduct themselves in an impeccably careful manner.

Sometimes the member of staff takes advantage of his or her new-found status and power and is duly resented. Tension and acrimony erupt and spread like tremors of an earthquake. It is safest to avoid all discussion of the matter except with your most trusted friends because gossip often returns to its subject. It is never wise to pass on anyone's comments because teachers who do so are never trusted again.

The powershift

The most difficult time to cope with staff politics is during the first two years of a new head. A powershift means that some people go up, some go down and someone gets hurt. Teachers who were in favour with the previous head can lose their influence under the new one and suffer the indignity of finding that their status is severely undermined. If this happens to you, in later years, you have two choices, grin and bear it or leave. Staying and fighting to recover your influence is not an option. I knew a teacher who tried it, and her influence and respect from the staff disintegrated daily.

Some new heads manage to gain the respect and goodwill of their staff within a few weeks. Some drive out most of the staff in one or two years. Heads, who lack confidence, begin by populating the staff room with their own friends from past schools. This often builds up a 'them and us' atmosphere which can be so severe that teachers leave, even though they themselves are not being harassed. This in turn exacerbates the situation, because the head can then employ more of his/her own pals.

It is best to keep your head down in these circumstances. Try not to be associated with either group, especially the clique who are congregating around the head, because their friendship is usually quite shallow and association earns you the distrust of the rest of the staff.

The worst possible situation is when a teacher has used his or her influence and favour with the head to attack others. I knew one such teacher and, under a new head, he went straight out of favour while one of his former victims found favour and wreaked his vengeance. What goes around, comes around. There is a God.

There might be a teacher who bears grudges for months and even years and these are best avoided like a wasps' nest. It is never wise to let irritations stay with you because schools are heavily pressurized communities and mountains grow out of molehills if not smoothed over.

Large schools are easier to work in than small ones, because in a large building it is easier to avoid anyone whom you find difficult company.

All of this may be painting a dismal picture. This is not the aim. Many schools have a happy, friendly atmosphere, with a terrific head and mutually-supportive teachers who keep each other afloat and laughing through every pitfall and challenge.

10 Don't lose sight of the big picture

In the hurly-burly of every busy day, it can become easy to lose sight of the real world. It's a bit like being a housewife. The more hours you put into the job, the more you notice there is to do.

When heads want jobs done, they tend to ask the busy members of staff. Some teachers, driven by an innate, creative urge or just eagerness to succeed, become carried away and spend so much time on the job, they become too tired to enjoy anything outside work. Some fall victim to the 'willing horse' syndrome. Heads spot the most efficient and ambitious teachers and give them a disproportionally large burden of extra tasks. Don't fall for it. Learn to use the word no. Of course you can dress it up a bit with answers like:

- 'Sorry, I'm snowed under with...'
- 'Sorry, I really can't take on anything extra until I have finished...'
- 'Sorry, for the moment I really must make it my priority to...'

Your mind needs to escape from work to stay sane and allow you to return to school refreshed. I was most impressed when a young teacher, about to go abroad, told me that in his new school, teachers were encouraged to have an interesting hobby which had nothing to do with their work. I'm sure it would enhance the quality of life for all teachers if British schools adopted the same view.

You might join a night class of some activity you enjoy, preferably one which is totally different from work. Unless for something unavoidable like parents' night, try never to miss it because of school work.

It is worthwhile to stay in touch with past college friends, even if they are at the other end of the country. If they are teachers, you can encourage each other.

Some teachers go home late, feeling so tired that their social life gradually starts to disintegrate during the term time, especially the first term.

However busy you might be, making new friends ought to be a priority, especially if you have moved to a different part of the country. If you go out for an evening with colleagues, try not to spend too much time talking about school. You'll feel better afterwards if you have stimulated your brain with something else.

One way to keep your spirits up is always to have some little treat to which you can look forward, a trip to the theatre or cinema, a game of football, a massage or just a night in the pub.

If you think that working fifty or more hours per week is unreasonable for an NQT's salary, remember that your body and mind will adjust to the long hours and the following year will be much easier, because the work will be no longer new and daunting, and you will get through it more quickly. It's comforting to realize that stress levels usually subside in the second year because you know the ropes, and you are no longer worried that you may not pass your induction year. Also, if you are in the same year group, you will have lots of ready-made plans to re-use.

When your induction year is over

When you reach the end of your first year and pass, make sure you don't do more than three or four days of school work during the holidays. A day at the beginning to sort out your classroom and two or three days just before you return for the Inset days at the start of the new term is plenty.

Now is the time to reward yourself with as comfortable, relaxing or exciting, and as long a holiday as you can afford. That puts everything into perspective and reminds you that there is more to life than work. It also gives you strength to face the next year and a taste of how you would like to spend your holidays in the future.

Remember, we are now living in an age where the world is your oyster and teachers with their long summer holidays can take advantage of it more than most. You've had the stress and hard work. Now is the time to make up for it and spoil yourself. It is teaching's big advantage over other professions. You'll be amazed how uplifted you will feel after a few weeks of doing something completely different.

Some teachers get into gear as soon as the pupils disappear on the last afternoon and others return a few days before the start of the next term's Inset. In some staffrooms, the conversation sounds like it's a travel agent's shop at the end of term.

There are a number of companies which specialize in a huge variety of summer adventures. The Internet has plenty of websites to find a trip for every exotic taste and give you ideas on how to get the best out of holidays. And remember they apply all year round.

You can have a white Christmas and New Year ski-ing in Bulgaria, the Pyrenees or the Dolomites. There are holidays touring the east coast of Australia – snorkling, exploring the Barrier Reef, sailing, white water rafting, quad-biking. You can explore India's historic sites, its magical temples and idyllic beaches. It's all there, ready for the taking.

I have worked with teachers of all ages who have joined the Ramblers and found that going off in an unfamiliar group was a great way to drive all thoughts of education out of their heads and return them to their classrooms, full of energy and enthusiasm to face the challenges of another year.

Remember Easyjet www.easyjet.com and Ryanair www.ryanair.com all do cheap flights even during the school holidays, so think ahead and book up well in advance. When the trip is booked, it will make the light at the end of the tunnel seem larger and closer.

And of course, when you do return to school, you might like to seek out the nervous NQTs in your school to make them welcome and offer them some friendly support and encouragement.

Believe in yourself

So far, everything in this handbook has been aimed at giving teachers practical tips on coping with a wide range of every day issues. I have omitted to mention that one essential ingredient of self-belief.

Some years ago a few inspectors in California called together a group of about thirty teachers from all parts of the state. They welcomed them to the meeting telling them that they had done a comprehensive study of all the teachers in the state and selected them as the most competent and inspiring teachers in California.

They praised them exuberantly and thanked them for their tremendous contribution to the students and asked them to return to their schools and use their talents to inspire others in their schools. In the years that followed those teachers were monitored closely and their students had exam results which improved enormously and far exceeded the national average, and the teachers' careers went from strength to strength.

BUT... interestingly, the entire exercise had been a sham. Those teachers had not been selected for their brilliance and expertise. They had been selected at random for an experiment to be carried out on themselves.

They had left the initial meeting buoyed up with self-confidence and self-belief, which spurred them on to their ensuing success.

The moral of the tale is that whether you believe that you can or you cannot, you are probably right. If you believe in yourself you can reach for the sky and any teacher can do it.

I can only tell you that your destiny is in your own hands and urge you to go for it.

THE LAST WORD
IF (with apologies to Rudyard Kipling)

If you can keep your cool when all around are
losing theirs
And blaming it on the headmaster.
If you can cope with lost kids on school trips,
impromptu class assemblies
And playground fights, without disaster.

If you can face unpopularity and criticism
In order to put the blooming kids first.
If you can defend your colleagues when they're
wrong
Knowing you'll probably come out worst.

If you can laugh and start again
When all your work and efforts are brought to
nought.
If you can keep kids on your side when they know
you've not prepared your lesson as you ought.

If you can patiently explain the simplest principle
Again and again and again and again.
If you can sanction and reprimand and at the end
of the day
Still be regarded as a friend.

If you can persuade the kids to take SATs
seriously
Though you know they're just a farce.
If you can avoid telling the head
To shove his targets up his arse.

If you can encourage and keep on board, the child
who always fails
No matter how hard he tries.
If you can make them take pride in their place in
the league tables
Knowing they're just a government PR exercise.

If you can care about Ofsted enough to pass,
But not so much as to sink into depression.
If you can cope with disappointment and failure
Several times in swift succession.

If you can make your point and stand firm
In the face of opposition without aggression.
You will last until you are pensioned off, and
what's much more,
You will survive the teaching profession.

H A Bennett

Hazel Bennett

Hazel Bennett has taught in a wide variety of schools in London since 1973 and been a class teacher in each age-group from reception to year 6, and a support teacher in every year group from nursery to year 8. She has also taught in a special school, a secondary school, been a supply teacher, a peripatetic teacher and taught abroad.

She has acquired post-graduate qualifications while running a home, bringing up a child and working full-time.

Hazel also written articles for educational magazines and websites and has taken part in Teachers TV programmes.

You can read about Hazel and her books on www.hazelbennett.co.uk and www.edgware-books.co.uk

Books by Hazel Bennett

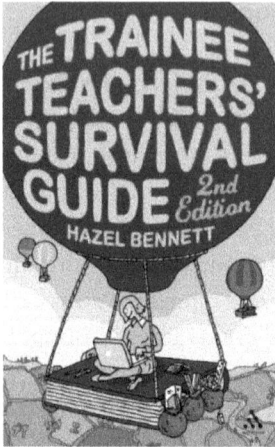

The Trainee Teachers' Survival Guide

Continuum International

ISBN 978 1 84706 056 3
First published in April 2006,

2nd Edition 2009

Teacher training has a high drop-out rate and this does not help a profession which has a shortage of members in some areas. This manual aims to guide student teachers and encourage them to keep going through their college work and teaching practices and finding their first job.

It is written sensitively to reassure students that they can rise above the difficulties and go on confidently to be successful teachers.

'The Trainee Teachers' Survival Guide' covers just about everything someone contemplating or undertaking a PGCE course could want to know... The sections on reflective practice, parents' evenings and balancing teaching with a family are particularly useful.'

Sarah Bubb, Times Educational Supplement. 1st Edition.

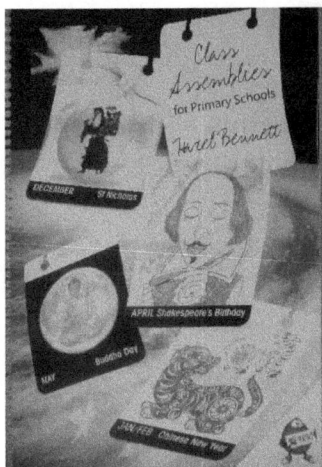

Class Assemblies for Primary Schools

Published in April 2007 by Educational Printing Services,
ISBN 1 905637 14 4
   Includes the right for the owner to photocopy.
Available at
enquires@eprint.co.uk

This wide-ranging and practical multicultural book includes a chapter on tips for presenting successful assemblies, followed by 36 delightful scripts, for Key Stage 2 classes to perform. Written in a mixture of prose and humorous rhyme-and-mime verse, each playlet is designed to involve every member of the class in the speech and action.

'Superb scripts in which every child plays a valued role. The rhyming aspect motivates and excites the children, enhancing the confidence and esteem of all, resulting in an excellent performance.'

Rochelle Waghorn, class teacher, who has successfully used some of them.

'Hazel Bennett has produced a life saver...'

Henry Phillips   Prep School Magazine

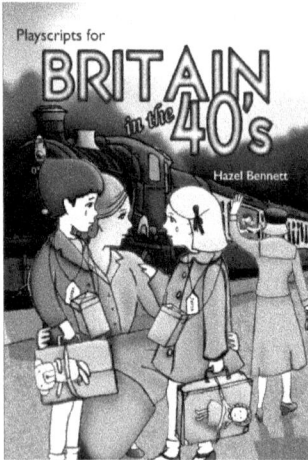

Playscripts for Britain in the 40s

Published by Educational Printing Services in 2008

ISBN 987 1 905637 41 6
Order online at
www.eprint.co.uk

This book of four playscripts is ideal for pupils in Key Stage 2, who are studying World War II and beyond. It explores the experience of war through the eyes of the people involved. Each story has a plot to engage the children's interest as they see how everyone coped with the hardships and upheavals, and rose above them.

Children, who are reluctant to read on their own, can enjoy reading the stories in a social group, while gaining an understanding of life in war-time Britain.

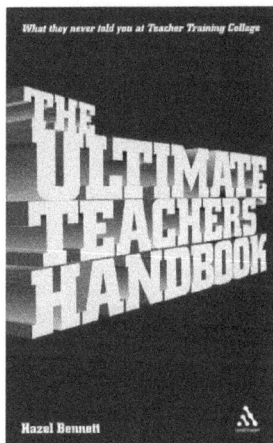

The Ultimate Teachers' Handbook

Published October 2005,
Continuum International,
ISBN 0 8264 8500 6

This is the definitive guide to surviving and succeeding in teaching. It covers all the things which teachers are not told at university but desperately need to know once they find themselves teaching full-time. It is humorously written, non-academic and jargon-free. It is now available in Chinese.

'This book publication reflects its title. It is powerful, informative and written in a non-ambiguous manner. It should be on all students' and NQTs' reading lists... Common sense, experience and effective ways of surviving in the school environment are combined in this excellently presented book.'
Len Parkyn   The Teacher   magazine of the NUT

'It's filled with very direct, useful and practical advice about everything from parent interviews, through seeking promotion, to taking assembly and surviving Ofsted. Unlike most books of its type, it recognises that teachers have a home life, which may include children of their own, to deal with.'
Gerald Haigh Times Educational Supplement

Appendix
Abbreviations

CD   Compact disk
CRB   Criminal Records Bureau
DfES   Department for Education and Skills
DVD   Digital versatile disk
EAL   English as an Additional Language
GCSE   General Certificate of Secondary Education
HLTA   Higher level teaching assistant
ICT   Information and Communications Technology
Inset   In-service education of teachers
KS   Key Stage
LEA   Local Education Authority
NQT   Newly qualified teacher
NC   National Curriculum
NFER   National Foundation for Educational Research
NQT   Newly qualified teacher
Ofsted   Office for Standards in Education
PE   Physical Education
PGCE   Post-Graduate Certificate in Education
PPA   planning, preparation and assessment
RE   Religious Education
SAT   Standardized Assessment Test
SEN   Special Educational Needs
SENCO   Special Educational Needs Co-ordinator
TES   Times Educational Supplement
QCA   Qualifications and Curriculum Authority
wpb   waste paper bin

Bibliography

Attwater, D. and John C. (1982), Dictionary of Saints
London: Penguin
Bennett, H. (2007) Class Assemblies for Primary Schools
Blackburn: Educational Printing Services
Children's Britannica Encyclopaedia Britannica
International Ltd, London.
Kidwell, V. (2004), Assemblies Made Easy. London:
Continuum International Publishing Group

Index

Whole chapters in **bold**